The

SEXUAL REVOLUTION

AND ITS

VICTIMS

35 PROPHETIC ARTICLES SPANNING TWO DECADES

JENNIFER ROBACK MORSE, PH.D

THE RUTH INSTITUTE

4845 LAKE STREET, SUITE 217
LAKE CHARLES, LA 70605
www.ruthinstitute.org \ 760-295-9278

v

Contents

CONTENTS

FOREWORD

When Ruth Institute Art Director, Todd Bingham, came up with the cover for this book, I knew the concept was perfect. Who better to represent the empty promises of the Sexual Revolution than Marilyn Monroe? She remains an iconic figure of sex appeal. When we see an image of her, we think Hollywood, and the power of feminine sexuality.

But there was a darker side to her life, a side so dark, we might well describe her life as tragic.

Marilyn Monroe's childhood included: a mentally unstable mother, a completely absent father, a disorganized childhood that included two different foster homes, probably sexual assault at the hands of adults in those homes, and an early marriage that she hoped would create stability. The "glamorous" bright side of her adult life included movie stardom, modeling, appearance in the first issue of Playboy in December 1953, three marriages, and an uncertain number of affairs. The dark side of her adult life included sexual exploitation by rich and powerful men, drug use, and her own cavalier disregard for the feelings of others. And in spite of all her fame and success, she had an unsureness of herself and her own value that included stage fright and finally, an early death.

Her life and death is a metaphor for the Sexual Revolution. The "glamour" and the empty promises get the full attention of the media. The downsides, not so much. The sexual exploitation that led to so much of the tragedy of Marilyn Monroe's life does not get the blame that it deserves. Neither does the brokenness of her early family life. We just keep looking at the carefully-crafted images and ignore the dark underside.

Likewise, the media still do not connect the dots between the poisonous ideology of the Sexual Revolution and the pain and grief and, ultimately, the loneliness that are endemic in our society.

This book tries to fill that gap.

The Sexual Revolution and its Victims is a series of essays I have written over 20 years. The first essay was published in the Harvard Journal of Law and Public Policy in 1995, when I was still a full-time economics professor. I was also trying to raise two small children, including one with special needs. The most recent material was composed especially for this book in the last days of 2014.

The process of writing these essays helped me clarify exactly what the Sexual Revolution is, what the alternative would look like and what we would need to do to create that alternative. The Introductory section has both a bright side and a dark side. In the opening essay, "I have a pro-life dream," I paint a picture of what the world would look like if the tenets of the Sexual Revolution were overturned. The "dark side" essay, "The New Class Warfare: All We Want to Do..." observes an important pattern in the political and rhetorical success of the Sexual Revolution.

In Section A, I dissect Sexual Revolutionary Propaganda. The rhetoric of the Sexual Revolution takes many deceptive twists and turns. Unraveling those twists and turns is a significant undertaking, which the casual reader or listener may not have the time or inclination to do. Each essay chooses a particular bit of rhetoric or a particular political ideological claim, and dissects it.

One particularly effective bit of propaganda is the redefinition of the term "freedom." The Revolutionaries have gained significant ground, simply by placing this venerable American concept into the service of their ideology. I unmask this process in Section B.

In the remaining sections of the book, I repeatedly propose this one idea: let us take a sober-minded look at the real costs of the Sexual Revolution. In one case after another, we see that things are not really as they seem. The costs are understated or completely ignored. The benefits of sexual license are overstated and glorified. All in all, it adds up to a perfect analogy for the airbrushed image of Marilyn Monroe. From abortion to contraception to cohabitation to the costs of divorce to the failures of sexual education, Americans have been fed a steady diet of half-truths.

These half-truths have contributed to making victims of us all. We participate in the Sexual Revolution, not fully realizing what we are getting ourselves into. Older and wiser people may advise us to slow down, but we are drawn by the glamour and the glitter. Only through sad experience do we learn for ourselves that our parents or grandparents were right.

This book represents twenty years of contemplation on these topics. The book is organized thematically, not chronologically. You will see the range of places in which I published these articles. You will intuit the range of places at which I gave speeches and seminars. I learned a great deal from my readers, and from my audiences. I am grateful to them all.

In my travels around the country, I talk with many people of all ages in my audiences. I receive emails daily from people who reso-nate with my skepticism about the Sexual Revolution. On radio talk shows, my callers confirm my sense that people are fed up with the Sexual Revolution. People are tired of being manipulated by the media, entertainment, academia and politicians. And it takes all of those groups of people working tirelessly together, to keep the myths of the Sexual Revolution alive.

I hope this book will bring clarity to your mind about these mat-ters. When I founded the Ruth Institute, I hoped to help young people "dodge the bullets" of some of the bad decisions that I made in my younger years. As I have continued this work, I realize that there are many people of my age group, who made similarly un-wise decisions. If you are one of these people, I want you to know that you are not alone! And I encourage you to speak out. You may think you are the only person who did something dumb. You may feel ashamed and want to keep to yourself.

But when half of marriages end in divorce, when 40% of children are born out of wedlock, when a quarter of pregnancies end in abortion, this is much more than a personal failing. This is evi-dence of a systemic problem. Do not blame yourself. I hope you will be inspired to see that your experience is not unique, that you are not alone. Most importantly, I hope you will see that your story has the potential to be helpful to someone else.

The Sexual Revolution keeps chugging along, because the Elites of our culture only tell half the story: the shiny glittering side of the story. But Marilyn Monroe did die a tragic and unnecessary death. Your story may help someone else avoid tragedy. I really encourage you to keep an open mind about this possibility. So many issues have been clouded by one-sided reporting and out-right propaganda. I have confidence that if people had the full story, they would make much better decisions.

I hope you will enjoy these essays! And come over and join us at the Ruth Institute! When you make it your business to inspire the survivors of the Sexual Revolution and expose the lies of the Sexual Revo-lution, you've always got something interesting to talk about!

Dr Jennifer Roback Morse

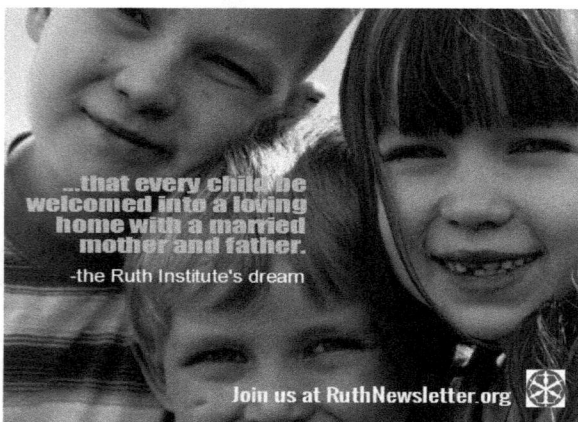

...that every child be welcomed into a loving home with a married mother and father.
-the Ruth Institute's dream

Join us at RuthNewsletter.org

~ 1 ~

I Have A (Pro-Life) Dream

Note to readers: During the last week of May 2006, I participated in an on-line debate at www.marriagedebate.com. My opponent was Christina Paige, author of "How the Pro-Choice Movement Saved America." In the course of that debate, she accused me of wanting to ban contraception. She said, "Don't tell me what you think is possible. Surely you have a dream." This is my response.

THANK YOU FOR ASKING. As a matter of fact, I do have a dream.

I have a dream that some day, every child will be conceived from an act of true love between parents who love each other, are married to each other, and eagerly welcome him. I have a dream that every child will spend his childhood with those parents who brought him into being. Parents see the value of the small society they have created between themselves and their children, and do everything humanly possible to sustain that society.

I have a dream that children can be children, take joy in their childhood innocence, and not become sexualized before puberty. All of society recognizes parents as the primary educators of their children, instead of regarding parents as impediments to formal sex education. Parents take seriously their responsibility to provide their children with accurate and complete information about sexuality, including the social and moral significance of sex, rather than acquiesce in whatever the school provides. Instead of the school deciding when children are ready for sexual information, parents monitor their child's maturity level, and make a considered judgment about when their child is ready. Parents feel themselves negligent if they fail in this. I have a dream that when parents elect to remove their children from public school sex ed classes, the parents no longer feel like interlopers and the children like outcasts.

I have a dream that Corporate America takes some responsibility for preserving the innocence of the young, and monitors the sexual images they place into the public square.

INTRODUCTION

Advertisers think it disreputable to market to children using sexual images. Retailers think it irresponsible to place erotic material at check-out counters and other places where children might stumble across them. The entertainment industry takes responsibility for limiting the sexual content of its programming to appropriate venues.

I have a dream that the market accommodates the needs of the family, rather than the family adapting itself to the needs of the market. We create an economy in which people are prepared to earn a living before the age of twenty-five or thirty. Young people graduate from college without crushing debt, and without the prospect of unmanageable housing costs and tax burdens. Families can support themselves on one income, at least for a while. Mothers can return to the labor market and find a place where they can use their talents and earn some money.

I have a dream that young women find a way to embrace their desire for motherhood as well as their desire for meaningful work outside the home. At some time in their lives, most women have the opportunity to give themselves over completely to caring for their children and making their home. Women make sensible life plans for themselves, that take into account the possibility that their children may be too needy to be in day care and may need to be with their mothers. I have a dream that mothers not feel that they are wasting themselves if they stay home with their children.

I have a dream that fathers and mothers are husbands and wives. Men and women learn to cooperate with each other, respect each other's differences, appreciate each other's unique gifts. Women can trust their husbands not to abandon them, and men can trust their wives not to eject them from the family home.

I have a dream that if a woman chooses a lifetime of barrier-free, chemical-free intimacy with her husband, she not be made to feel like a freak. A family with many children can appear in public, without having to endure rude remarks. People might even show some gratitude to those who are investing their lives and their bodies in building the future of society.

And if any of these things are not possible for a young couple, I have a dream that friends and family will step up to help them. We find a way to accommodate and assist people who are unable to live up to the social norms, without destroying or dissipating those norms. Neighbors will help see them through their difficulties. And if it must be that they rely on the kindness of strangers, these strangers become friends.

I have a dream that we recognize that we have been trying to do something that no society in the history of the human race has ever attempted: create a society that has no norms at all about the proper context for sexual activity or childbearing. We come to recognize how unlikely this is to succeed.

So you see, I am not being evasive when I say I have no interest in regulating contraception. I believe that the widespread pro- motion of contraception has unleashed many social forces that would have been best contained. But it does not follow that the way to improve our situation is to retrace our steps. I realize that my agenda is not modest. Yet many changes I support do not involve legislation or regulation at all, but rather changes in private-sector policies that accompany a change of heart. Among those that do require government action, such as reform of di- vorce laws, the most appropriate venue is state or local legisla- tion, not dictates from the federal judiciary.

You accuse me of wanting to turn back the clock to the 1950's. I have no desire to go backwards. If we are going to go back to any place, it might as well be the Garden of Eden. That is where we are all trying to go anyway, and it is just as practical as going back to the Eisenhower Administration.

No, I do not want to go back anywhere. I want us to go forward, to become what we should have been from the beginning.

Originally published: Townhall
May 1, 2006

Available on-line at: http://townhall.com/columnists/jenniferrobackmorse/2006/05/01/i_have_a_ pro-life_dream/page/full

~ 2 ~

The New Class Warfare: "All we want to do..."

ALLOW ME TO POINT out a pattern in the promotion of the Sexual Revolution:

All we want to do is lower the cost of divorce to the handful of people whose marriages have irretrievably broken down. All we want to do is allow abortion for cases of rape and incest.

OH, NO....NOT AGAIN!

All we want to do is allow married couples to use contraception for serious health reasons.

All we want to do is provide sexual education for children whose parents might not be responsible enough to do it themselves.

All we want to do is allow underage girls to get abortions and contraception without their parents knowing, because some parents might abuse the girl.

Never mentioned in any of these historical episodes, is the fact that the purveyors of these lines are simply lying. They want more, much more, than they are admitting. They know exactly what they are planning to do. They have other, much more extensive purposes than they will admit in public.

They know perfectly well that the public would not accept their larger purpose. They know perfectly well that once the principle is established in law and social practice, it is much easier to expand the application of that principle into more extensive areas of life. They know perfectly well that the public would not accept the larger agenda because that more extensive agenda has problems hidden beneath the surface.

Out in front of all these "modest reform" campaigns is the battle cry of freedom. "All we want to do is allow people the opportunity, the freedom, to make their own choices about their lives."

Never mind whether we plan to give them full access to the information that would allow meaningful choice.

Never mind that we plan to systematically underestimate the down-side of participating in the Sexual Revolution, while systematically overestimating the benefits.

Never mind whether the choices we are steering people towards even have a remote chance of turning out as promised.

No, as long as we can allow people to go through the motions of making their own decisions, it does not matter how much we manipulate the conditions of their choice-making.

We, the Ruling Class, will never, never mention the fact that we have the resources to buy our way out of the trouble and the problems these liberties caused for us. In fact, we will never, never admit that there ever were any such troubles or problems.

We, the Ruling Class, will never, never notice the fact that those of modest means, the poor, the working class, even the modestly middle class, cannot buy their way out of these troubles. But in fact, the side effects from the Sexual Revolution devastated the lives of anyone outside our social class.

We, the Ruling Class, will never, never mention the members of our social class who are making money off of the misery of the poor and working class whose family lives have fallen apart.

And now they tell us, "All we want to do is allow two people of the same sex who love each other to get married."

Do they really expect us to believe that this is all they want? Seriously?

I don't know about you, but I'm not buying it.

Originally published: Ruth Blog
June 25, 2014

Available on-line at: http://www.ruthblog.org/2014/06/25/the-new-class-warfare-all-we-want-to-do/

SECTION A:
DISSECTING
PROPAGANDA

~ 3 ~

Dissecting Sexual Revolutionary Propaganda

AS I HAVE SAID many times in my speeches (available at the Ruth Institute podcast page), the Sexual Revolution is irrational and its goals are impossible. Therefore, those committed to the Sexual Revolution must also commit themselves to a steady stream of propaganda to over-write the basic facts of reality. This sometimes includes the subtle or not-so-subtle rewriting of history.

Today's exhibit in understanding Revolutionary Propaganda comes to us from the Religion News Service, which describes itself this way.

"The Religion News Service aims to be the largest single source of news about religion, spirituality and ideas. We strive to inform, illuminate and inspire public discourse on matters relating to belief and convictions."

So I find it odd, to say the least, to find an organization with this mission, taking for granted the arguments of Sexual Revolutionaries in an article, described as an "analysis."

Let me confine myself to one particularly noticeable re-writing of history.

Written by Kevin Eckstrom, the Editor in Chief of the Religion News Service, the article claims in the section called, "A problem of overreach:"

"Conservative groups resisted moves to compromise on a half-measure like civil unions; (Tony) Perkins' organization (Family Research Council) calls civil unions nothing more than 'a slow-motion surrender.' And that, said veteran gay marriage proponent Jonathan Rauch, was a critical mistake."

The author provides no context for cultural conservative Perkins' comment, and he gives pro-gay Jonathan Rauch the last word. By doing this, the author suggests that Perkins' assessment is incorrect, without actually taking responsibility for proving this, or even stating that his assessment is incorrect.

However, a small amount of research would show that Perkins' analysis was correct. A reasonable observer would conclude from the behavior of the Gay Lobby that they do indeed regard civil unions as stepping stones, not compromises.

Consider California. Very ample domestic partnership provisions were in place by September 2003. (Same sex couples have had hospital visitation rights in California since AB 26 passed in 1999.) But domestic partnerships, solving virtually all of the practical problems that same sex couples might encounter, were not good enough for the Gay Lobby.

In February 2004, San Francisco mayor Gavin Newsom issued marriage licenses to same sex couples in his city. This began the process that led to the *in re Marriage* cases, which overturned the statute defining marriage as the union of a man and a woman.

Only after observing the progress of that lawsuit through the courts, did the people of California put Prop 8 on the ballot in 2008, as a defensive measure. In retrospect, an honest observer might think the advocates of natural marriage were overly naïve and too passive. But Religion News Service Editor-in-chief Kevin Eckstrom reports Jonathan Rauch's opinion as if it were the Gospel Truth.

"They (cultural conservatives) set an impossible goal for themselves by saying from day one that the goal of success would be not one gay marriage on not one square inch of American soil, and that was never going to happen."

Who? Who ever said "not one gay marriage on not one square inch of American soil?" And after the Gay Lobby went for "the whole enchilada" of gay "marriage" less than six months after the passage of sweeping domestic partnership benefits, why should any reasonable person believe that compromise was possible?

I don't know what Kevin Eckstrom believes in his heart of hearts. I don't know whether he is a Dupe or a Useful Idiot or was just careless on this particular day. But one cannot escape the conclusion, that wittingly or unwittingly, this uncritical reporting of conservative "overreach" is not news, and certainly not "religion" news. Rather, it is an attempt to rewrite history in accordance with the narrative of the Gay Lobby.

Originally published: Ruth Blog
May 29, 2014

Available on-line at: http://www.ruthblog.org/2014/05/29/dissecting-sexual-revolutionary-propaganda/

SECTION A
DISSECTING PROPAGANDA

~ 4 ~

Reflections of a Former Fetus and Former Incubator

RADICAL PRO-CHOICE RHETORIC ATTACKS the most basic facts of our human existence: that the human body comes in two different but complementary types, male and female. They cannot forgive women who embrace femininity rather than neuter themselves.

They were out in force at the San Francisco Walk for Life, the couple hundred pro-abortion leftists protesting the fifty thousand of us who came to walk for life. The Stop Patriarchy group met us at 5th and Market Street, carrying signs saying, "Abortion on Demand and Without Apology."

You might think a group like this is so radical that they don't matter. But looking closely at radicals helps us see the root of a set of ideas, ideas held by more mainstream people who appear less threatening. Considering Stop Patriarchy's rhetorical strategy also reveals how such an irrational set of ideas has advanced so far. They lead with something unobjectionable, and then segue into something far more sinister.

Their website reveals that they attack pornography. So far, so good. (If you do visit their website, be advised: I have edited out some of the more vulgar phrases in my quotations.) Here's an excerpt:

"In recent years, pornography has become increasingly violent, cruel, degrading towards women; . . . Meanwhile, the broader culture has been pornified: pole dancing is taught at gyms, "sexting" is a national phenomenon among teens, and the strip club is the accepted backdrop to "male bonding." All this is tied in with, and reinforces, the trafficking of millions of women and girls as literal chattel in the international sex industry.

This is NOT society becoming more comfortable with sex. This is society becoming saturated with the sexualized degradation of women. (emphasis in original)"

Pornography degrades women. I can go along with that. Every serious Catholic and Christian I know can go along with that. John Paul II would go along with that. In fact, he said, "the

27

problem with pornography is not that it shows too much of a human person, but that it shows too little." I know Mormons and Evangelicals who are working to put a stop to the degradation of women through the pornography industry and sex trafficking.

The Stop Patriarchy people are quite correct to condemn pornography and to work to end it. This is the unobjectionable, even noble, first move. The next move is more questionable.

"A Christian fundamentalist-driven assault is imperiling abortion, birth control, real sex education and women's lives. Lesbian, gay, bisexual and transgendered (LGBT) people who do not conform to traditional patriarchal gender and sexual norms are demonized and threatened. Abortion doctors are killed. Women who seek abortions—or even birth control—are stigmatized. 2011 saw the largest spate of legal restrictions on abortion since Roe v. Wade in 1973.

ALL THIS MUST BE STOPPED!

Fetuses are not babies. Women are not incubators. Abortion is not murder. (emphasis in original)"

A world without abortion is in their minds the equivalent of a world saturated with pornography. The people at Stop Patriarchy do not seem to realize that the promise of sex without babies is one of the biggest cultural tailwinds pushing the whole pornography industry along. Where would pornographers be without contraception and legal abortion?

The presence of a new baby or a pregnant woman would certainly mess up the storyline (I use the term loosely) of the typical porn film. Outside the porn industry, contraception with abortion as a backup delivers women to men for their use. Separating sex from conception removes constraints and responsibilities from men, and invites them to use women as objects. This is just as Paul VI predicted in *Humanae Vitae,* back in 1968.

I cannot recall a single one of the fifty thousand of us at the San Francisco Walk for Life saying or implying that "women are incubators." No one in the "Patriarchy" of the hierarchy of the Catholic Church refers to women in such degrading terms. Only the members of Stop Patriarchy demean women in this way.

Here is the "money quote," where Stop Patriarchy pivots from promoting something entirely unobjectionable (the end of pornography) to something entirely destructive.

"Women are not objects. Women are not things to be used for the sexual pleasure of men NOR are they breeders of children. WOMEN ARE HUMAN BEINGS CAPABLE OF FULL EQUALITY IN EVERY REALM! (emphasis in original)"

These lines give a window into the soul of the Stop Patriarchy movement. Their claim here is that being "breeders of children" is the opposite of "women are human beings capable of full equality in every realm!" The term "breeder" is a term of degradation, a demeaning term, a term that says that mothers are somehow less than fully equal with men, or with other women. Being a mere "breeder" keeps us women from "full equality in every realm."

Once you actually analyze it, this is an astounding thought.

The simple honest-to-goodness truth is that men and women are different. Giving birth to a child highlights the differences between men and women. Men and women do not become parents in the same way. Men and women feel differently about parenthood, and do parenthood differently. Motherhood has a different impact on women than fatherhood has on men.

These differences, generated by our bodies, in how we experience parenthood are among the most basic facts about our species. But, in the minds of Stop Patriarchy, these very differences between men and women are themselves injustices.

We can see now why this type of leftist is always so angry. It is impossible for them to achieve their objectives. They are always frustrated. We can see now, also, why they are never satisfied, no matter how many benefits they obtain for women, no matter how revolutionary the changes they obtain. In their minds, even a ten-dollar copay for contraception is the residue of the cosmic conspiracy against women's "humanity" and their "full equality in every realm."

It is completely bizarre to treat motherhood as the moral equivalent of rape or pornography. Yet that is exactly the parallel that Stop Patriarchy sets up in its rhetoric and its demands. In their minds, being a "breeder of children"—a sneering synonym for women's natural ability to bring new life into the world—is somehow the same as being a "thing to be used for the pleasure of men."

Stop Patriarchy's ultimate problem is not really with capitalism or even with violence. Their problem is with the human body.

29

They resent the fact that the human body comes in two different but complementary types, male and female. They are angry that childbearing impacts men and women differently. They resent every social structure and every human feeling that depends on the male-female differentiation. They cannot forgive women like me, who embrace femininity rather than neuter themselves at their urging.

This is why it is correct to identify them as revolutionaries. They are in revolt against the embodied nature of the human person. They hate sexual differentiation, maleness and femaleness.

Male and female are two equally beautiful but different ways of being human. If we lose our ability to fully embrace our manhood or our womanhood, we lose our ability to be human.

Make no mistake about it. An attack on sexual differentiation is an attack on the human body. An attack on the human body is an attack on the human race.

But the people of Stop Patriarchy cannot stop themselves. Once convinced of their opening premise, they have no choice but to try to suppress all the differences between men and women. Everything that has to do with reproduction must be suppressed or neutralized.

The goal is clear: The only good woman is a neutered woman. The only good man is a gay man, who poses no sexual threat to women. The only good child is a chosen child. They do not seem to realize that this commodifies the child, making him or her an object to obtain if we want one, and a problem to solve if we don't want one. Nor do they seem to realize that today's young people intuit this, which is why so many of the Walkers for Life carried signs saying, "I am the Pro-Life Generation."

We may be tempted to "click away" from Stop Patriarchy and ignore them as obviously deluded people who shouldn't be taken seriously. But that would be a mistake. For this very same thought pattern lies behind the HHS contraceptive mandate and the War on Women rhetoric promoted by the political party now in power. And the party out of power seems either unwilling or unable to confront the ideology for what it is: the ideology of a totalitarian movement, bent on denying and wiping out the most basic facts of our human experience.

We should cut no slack, give no quarter, concede no ground, to these enemies of the human race. Not out of politeness, nor out of courtesy, and certainly, not out of fear. Ignoring people because they are irrational has probably been one of our biggest tactical mistakes. Though Stop Patriarchy's irrationality makes them hard to argue with, they are deadly serious, and we need to be as well.

Originally published: The Public Discourse
February 1, 2013

Available on-line at: http://www.thepublicdiscourse.com/2013/02/7823/ - Reprinted with permission

31

~ 5 ~

Marching on the Right Side of History

D EFENDERS OF MARRIAGE SHOULD draw hope and courage from the pro-life movement's success.

As an advocate of conjugal marriage, I am often told that I am on the "Wrong side of History." The justice of "marriage equality" is overwhelming; the younger generation favors it; same sex marriage is inevitable. But this analysis is false. Indeed, there is ample reason to think that the March of History storyline will be proven incorrect. The reason? We were told all these same things about abortion.

"You need to accept *Roe v. Wade*. The unlimited abortion license is nothing but simple justice for women. Besides, the next generation will completely accept abortion. They will grow up knowing nothing else. They will not have all your hang-ups about sex and your squeamishness about scraping a bit of tissue out of a woman's body. Reproductive freedom is the wave of the future. You are on the Wrong Side of History."

A funny thing happened on the way to History: the people did not perform as promised. Last year, I took a group of Ruth Institute students up to the West Coast Walk for Life in San Francisco. Official estimates place the attendance at over 35,000. But I wasn't counting. I was looking at the faces. I saw what anyone can see, if they care to look: the pro-life movement is a youth movement.

The average age of the walkers at the West Coast Walk for Life was probably around late twenties, and even lower if you count babies in strollers. Toward the front of the parade were the Berkeley Students for Life (yes, there is such a thing) and the Stanford pro-life club, (yes, they exist as well), their long-standing cross-Bay rivalry set aside for the day. Busloads of high school students, college students road-tripping in from all over the West Coast, whole church youth groups, families with small children, babies in arms, backpacks and strollers. The next generation is not going along quietly with the Inexorable March of History.

And why should they?

The pro-abortion forces did not correctly predict how the young would react to the Abortion Regime. Simple demographics favor a pro-life next generation: advocates of life have more children on average than their opponents. But beyond that, every person under the age of 38 is in some sense a survivor of the abortion regime. Any of them could have been killed. And some of them realize that.

Many of them have seen friends have abortions to save relationships with boyfriends, only to have the boyfriend end the relationship anyway. Some of them have learned from experience that recreational sex is not as fun as they imagined. The coarsening of sexual relationships, the pressure on women to perform sexually, the easy escape for men from responsibility for their unborn children: some of the Millennials have put two and two together and figured out that the abortion regime enables all this.

Katelyn Sills, President of Berkeley Students for Life, attended the 2011 Walk on Saturday. She reports that the pro-life initiative comes from the young people themselves, not from their parents or other authority figures. When high school students form a pro-life club, it isn't to pad their resumes: that particular extra-curricular activity won't impress most college admissions offices. Students form pro-life clubs because they see the injustice of abortion: they identify with the child.

It is the interests of children that the Abortion Regime set aside in order to accommodate the desires of adults. And it is the interests of children that the redefinition of marriage is in the process of setting aside as well. Remember the old pro-abortion slogan, "every child a wanted child?" Who can take that seriously today? "Kids just need two adults who love them" will come to sound every bit as hollow.

Same-sex civil marriage tacitly but surely asserts that kids don't really need mothers and fathers, and that mothers and fathers are interchangeable. The next generation will grow up with the consequences of institutionalizing this belief throughout society. Same-sex civil marriage is turning the drift toward artificial reproductive technology for infertile married couples into a tidal wave of entitlement for anyone married or single, straight or gay, of any age, to manufacture children for any reason. Redefining marriage will come to mean that there is no particular reason to insist on two parents. Some in the next generation will have three or four parents.

Advocates of redefining marriage assure us that all will be well. Children will do fine, whatever the loving adults in their lives decide to do. IVF children will be so wanted by their legal parents

34

that the lifetime separation from their natural parents will not trouble them. And children of unconventional family structures will have more adults to love them. Divorce, separation, complex custody quarrels, kids shuttling between four households with their sleeping bags and backpacks: that's just anti-equality hysteria and will never happen.

As time goes on, it will become more obvious that "marriage equality" requires us, men, women and children alike, to ignore biology. Some women who have children with female partners will find that sharing the care of her child with another woman, is not the same as sharing the care of her child with the child's father. Some men who agree to be sperm donors as "friends" will find that they want more of a relationship with their own children than they had anticipated. And some children are going to have feelings about their absent parents, uncomfortable questions about their origins, and complex emotions about being partially purchased.

Advocates of same sex marriage typically respond, "That's just biology," as if biology were nothing. These advocates are asking people to set aside the natural attachment of parents to their own children, the natural difficulties of treating another person's child as if they were your own, the natural desires of children to know who they are and where they came from. And these advocates are asking the whole of society to ignore sexual differentiation in parenthood: no mothers, no fathers, just generic parents. These enemies of the human body seem to forget that there are no generic people, just men and women.

As acceptance of gender-neutral marriage spreads throughout society, some same sex couples will not be "gay:" they will be forming same sex unions of convenience. And even among the gays and lesbians who marry, not all of them will be the most committed ideologues. Some will just want to live the ordinary lives that advocates of same sex marriage have been promising them. But biology will assert itself.

Children with father-hunger will start to speak up. Young people will start to notice that some of the differences between men and women actually matter. Mothers in same sex unions will start to notice that raising sons without fathers is harder than they had been led to believe. Suppressing all these feelings in all these people will simply not be possible indefinitely. Not everyone will remain silent. Abortion advocates never anticipated the Silent No More campaign, wherein women suffering the after-effects of their abortions began to speak up. As time marches on, the brutality of the marriage "equality" regime will become just as obvious as the brutality of the abortion regime is today.

The children themselves will eventually have something to say about all this. Today, the energy and enthusiasm of the young is on the side of life. And in spite of everything we hear today, the same will be true of natural marriage. Conjugal marriage is the Right Side of History.

Originally published: The Public Discourse
January 24, 2011

Available on-line at: http://www.thepublicdiscourse.com/2011/01/2439/ - Reprinted with permission

~ 6 ~

Does Marriage End Poverty?

NOW THAT THE REPUBLICAN CONSULTANTS[1] ARE waking up and seeing that marriage matters, the "Progressives" are reacting precisely on cue, for instance, with this story: "Promoting marriage among single mothers: An ineffective weapon in the war on poverty?"[2] The Usual Suspects discover that urging people to get married won't solve all their poverty problems. But when you actually drill down and read the story, you see that they are actually conceding a great deal to the case for natural marriage as the proper context for both sex and childbearing.

The reason getting married doesn't solve the problems low income women face is simple: many low income women have already made seriously bad choices in partners when they had their first child, and before they got married. According to the definitive Fragile Families study,[3] low income unmarried mothers seldom marry the father of their first child. When an unmarried couple has a child, only 16% of them eventually get married to each other and are still married 5 years after the birth of their child.

Interestingly enough, the second or later relationships tend to be with "better" partners. For instance they are more likely to be high school graduates, more likely to be employed, less likely to be violent or have a criminal record or be a drug abuser. This suggests that the mothers are learning from their experiences with less desirable men.

But why do they have to learn everything on their own? What would be so wrong with a social support system that steers people away from making these early, disastrous mistakes? In other words, what would be so wrong with taking as normative, the idea that sex and children and marriage all go together. Don't

1 Ari Fleischer, "How to Fight Income Inequality: Get Married," **Wall Street Journal,** January 12, 2014, available on-line at http://www.wsj.com/news/ articles/SB10001424052702304325004579296752404877612
2 Kristi Williams, "Promoting marriage among single mothers: An ineffective weapon in the war on poverty?," **Council on Contemporary Families,** January 6, 2014, available on-line at: https://contemporaryfamilies.org/marriage-ineffective-in-war-on-poverty-report/
3 Sara McLanahan, "Fragile Families and the Reproduction of Poverty," **Annals of the American Academy of Political Social Science,** Jan 1, 2009; 621(1): 111–131.http://www.ncbi.nlm.nih.gov/pmc/articles/PMC2831755/

have sex with someone who would be a disaster to be married to. Postpone age at first intercourse. Find a good partner. Then, get married and have sex. Then have babies.

That would seriously interrupt the whole Sex Positive ideological storyline that sex has nothing to do with babies, and that marriage is optional.

The bottom line of the Fragile Families Study points to the significant role played by the decisions around marriage and childbearing.

> Most importantly, none of these (suggested policies, including job training, tax programs, etc.) programs is likely to have a large effect as long as mothers continue to have children before they find a long term partner. Although wage subsidies and relationship counseling may ameliorate some of the problems associated with non-marital childbearing, they are likely to be limited in what they can accomplish. Thus, in order to break the intergenerational cycle of poverty, we will need to find a way to persuade young women from disadvantaged backgrounds that delaying fertility while they search for a suitable partner will have a payoff that is large enough to offset the loss of time spent as a mother or the possibility of forgoing motherhood entirely.

To do that, it would be really helpful if the Elites of this culture would abandon their ideological system that says that sex is a recreational activity that is normatively sterile, and that marriage is a trap that no self-respecting woman should have anything to do with. (Unless she is a lesbian, in which case, marriage is absolutely essential to her well-being. But I digress.)

Low income women involved in multi-partner fertility are victims of the Sexual Revolution, the preferred ideology of the Elites of all parties.

Originally published: Ruth blog
January 14, 2014
(Under the title, "Now that Republican Consultants are waking up to the marriage issue....")

Available on-line: http://www.ruthblog.org/2014/01/14/now-that-republican-consultants-are-waking-up-to-the-marriage-issue/

~ 7 ~

Getting Zapped for a Good Cause:
A Review of "Home Economics"

HAVE YOU EVER SEEN a dog race up to the boundary of a yard, and abruptly stop? It looks very odd, until you realize that the dog is wearing a fancy collar. There is an invisible electric "fence" embedded in the yard. The dog has been shocked so often that it stops before actually touching the invisible fence line.

This image flashed in my mind as I was reading *Home Economics: The Consequences of Changing Family Structure,* by Nick Schulz of the American Enterprise Institute. Mr. Schulz does a fine job laying out the harmful effects of the deconstruction of the family on individuals, the economy and the larger project of the free society. But he studiously avoids anything that might have even the remotest chance of "zapping" him with the label of "moralizing."

It's an odd position to take—the avoidance of moralizing—considering how destructive are the trends tracked in the book. I should think we would all wish to condemn vigorously something we knew to be harmful to large numbers of people, especially the poor and uneducated.

The family trends are, by now, pretty well-known. Fewer people are getting married and staying married. More people are cohabiting. More children are born out of wedlock.

The disastrous consequences of these trends are well-known too. Higher probability of social pathologies. Lower levels of human and social "capital" for the children born into unmarried or unstable households. Bigger problems for the lower classes than for the educated classes.

Experts are also even aware of this politically incorrect fact: The family behavior of the educated classes is pretty much the same as the people of those dreaded fifties, with low levels of divorce and non-marital childbearing. The major difference between these two demographics is that today's educated couples start their fami-

39

lies almost ten years later than June and Ward Cleaver would. Given that this is all well-known, why did the American Enterprise Institute see the need to recount these facts? True, Mr. Schulz ties them together with the economic thread: family breakdown is bad for the economy. But even this is well-known. I said it back in 2001, in Love and Economics.[1]

So, why write about a well-known social trend that is well-known to be destructive, and then studiously avoid moralizing? This is, to me, the interesting question raised by this compact book. Mr. Schulz gives a clue as to what he fears when he quotes a young female blogger, who dismissively refers to some unnamed people who wish to "restore the patriarchy to a perceived '50s-era hey-day."

I find it instructive that Mr. Schulz chooses to include this comment in his own book. He does not attempt to challenge or refute it. He merely calls it "interesting."

I believe this comment is his way of throwing out the obligatory protective covering, when he promises to refrain from "passing judgment about divorce or out-of-wedlock births." I suppose he, and his boss at AEI, are hoping that the data will speak for itself. If we just put out enough data, often enough, every reasonable person will draw the conclusion that we should discourage divorce and out-of-wedlock births. Or at the very least, we should refrain from encouraging these behaviors.

I would like to say to Mr. Schulz: You need not appease the moralizing self-described "feminists." They aren't speaking for all women. They are certainly not speaking for all mothers. And, let's get real: They are moralizing all over the place.

Let's review the female blogger's slur against those unnamed people who would: "restore the patriarchy to a perceived '50s-era." In less than ten words, she blasts out an amorphous blob of disapproval. The fact that she is not too specific about what she is saying is very important. That way, she does not actually have to prove or disprove anything. She makes tacit moral arguments and implicit empirical claims. But since you don't know what those arguments and claims actually are, she doesn't have to defend them.

While the argument is tacit, the moral disapproval she conveys

---

1   The subtitle to this book was originally, **"The Laissez Faire Family Doesn't Work."** Dr. Morse changed it with the second edition, to: "It Takes a family to Raise a Village."

is quite explicit. Anyone who disagrees with her not-very-specific point is morally defective. Everyone gets the picture that they're not to be on the side of the fearsome "patriarchy," or defend the dreaded "fifties."

Zap! This is the invisible electric fence. Don't say anything negative about out-of-wedlock births or divorce, or you will get a shock!

Some of the sources Mr. Schulz quotes use the passive language so typical of the discussion around the social issues. For instance, he quotes one study called "The Decline of Marriage and the Rise of New Families."

This language is designed to convey the notion that no one took any actions that caused marriage to "decline" or the "new families" to "rise." These things happened on their own, like so many forces of nature.

Or how about this line: "Some scholars argue that in the past five decades, the basic architecture of these age-old institutions has changed as rapidly as at any time in human history." No one is responsible. The institutions just "changed."

Really? All by themselves.

No human agency is involved whatsoever. Only the mindless inevitable March of History.

The fact is that particular people advocated particular policies, both public and private, that led to these behavioral changes. The fact is we could make some policy changes—if we really wanted to—that would be very helpful and not particularly intrusive.

For instance, the government could do something about out-of-wedlock births by ceasing to promote artificial contraception.

Zap! Dr. Morse, how could you say such a thing?

Yes, you heard me. And yes, you know I'm right. The widespread practices of contraception and abortion have gone hand-in-hand with the rise of out-of-wedlock childbearing. That's because acting as if sex is a sterile activity will lead people to have sex when they cannot possibly sustain a pregnancy. When these pregnancies occur, as they inevitably will since no contraceptive is perfect, the woman in the impossible situation will either abort the child or become a single mom.

Mr. Schulz quotes one particularly shocking statistic, which reveals far more than he probably intended.

What percentage of never-married young adults use birth control

41

"every time" they have intercourse?

According to Figure 5-2 in the book, only 55% of "highly educated" young adults use contraceptives "every time." A mere 19% of the "least educated" use contraceptives "every time."

People don't use contraceptives "every time," despite its massive subsidy and promotion by the government.

Nevertheless, people still act as if sex is a sterile recreational activity.

(And people call me "unrealistic" for saying that the world would be a better place if people only had sex with the person to whom they were married. But I digress.)

Ergo, the government should stop promoting contraception. Let people use it if they want to. But stop trying to create a world where sex is sterile. It can't be done.

We could do something about the divorce rate.

Zap! Dr. Morse, have you lost your mind?

We could end the government policy of taking sides with the partner who least wants to be married. That is what "no-fault" or, more accurately, "unilateral" divorce does. The government enters into marital disputes on the side of the least committed partner.

The moratorium on moralizing benefits the people who are trying to keep a defensive wall around a set of policies that are morally indefensible.

Listen up, Mr. Schulz. You can get a good running start, and blast through the electric fence. It stops hurting once you get on the other side. It actually only stings for a minute.

So come on through with me. I ran through it a long time ago! And now that I'm outside that little fenced-in yard, I'm free.

Originally published: Ethika Politika
August 16, 2013

Available on-line at: http://ethikapolitika.org/2013/08/16/getting-zapped-for-a-good-cause-a-review-of-home-economics-the-consequences-of-changing-family-structure/ - Reprinted with permission

SECTION B
A DIFFERENT KIND
OF FREEDOM

~ 8 ~

The Illusions of Reproductive Freedom:
Part I

THE ASYMMETRY OF REPRODUCTIVE FREEDOM

THE FEMINIST ESTABLISHMENT IS in an uproar over the appointment of Judge John Roberts to replace retiring Justice
Sandra Day O'Connor. In their minds, the abortion license
established by *Roe v. Wade* is sacrosanct. But I believe the very
concept of reproductive freedom is a dangerous illusion that has
brought misery to millions of people. The series of Court cases
which created this illusion increased access to both contraception
and abortion. These cases did indeed, allow people to change the
probability of a live baby resulting from any sexual act. It would
be a defensible intellectual position to claim that people are entitled to use new technologies to change these probabilities. But
under feminist tutelage, the social norms and constitutional inter-
pretation around sex and conception have morphed into a much
stronger demand: We now believe that we are entitled to have sex
without having a live baby result.

But this is far less appealing than "the right to choose." The vari-
ous euphemisms such as "reproductive self-determination," and
"reproductive justice," vastly overstate what government can provide. The government cannot assure anyone that they will achieve
their reproductive goals. This so-called freedom is a negation: it
is only the right to say "no" to a baby.

CHANGED PROBABILITIES, NOT ABSOLUTE ENTITLEMENTS

In the 1972 case, *Eisenstadt v Baird,* the Supreme Court began
to exaggerate its capacities. This case broadened the right of unmarried individuals to have access to information about contraceptives. The Court stated:

"The marital couple...is an association of two individuals each
with a separate intellectual and emotional makeup. If the right
of privacy means anything, it is the right to be free from unwarranted government intrusions into matters so fundamentally af-
fecting a person as the decision whether to bear or beget a child."

Legal impediments to the flow of information may amount to

45

SECTION B
A DIFFERENT KIND OF FREEDOM

"unwarranted government intrusion," into an admittedly very personal decision; fair enough. However, allowing people full access to information does not completely remove all barriers to the personal decision of "whether to bear or beget a child." All the information in the world about the most sophisticated forms of contraception does not assure that a person will be able to fulfill their reproductive plans. Contraception sometimes fails. People sometimes use it incorrectly, or intermittently. In these cases, the person's "decision" to avoid conception will not be fully realized. It is not any state interference, warranted or unwarranted, that thwarted the person's "decision," but simply the probabilistic connection between sexual activity, contraception and conception.

So, the only way to avoid unwanted pregnancy while being sexually active is to have unlimited access to abortion. More accurately, I should say, this is the only way the state could guarantee the right to have sex without having a live baby. Perhaps it is not surprising that *Roe v. Wade* followed a mere year after *Eisenstadt*.

Affirming *Roe* in *Planned Parenthood of Southeastern Pennsylvania v. Casey* in 1992, the Court continued this overstatement of its powers.

"The ability of women to participate equally in the economic and social life of the Nation has been facilitated by their ability to control their reproductive lives...."

But the "control of their reproductive lives" that the Court promises through *Roe* is only a negative right. The Court did not, and in the nature of things, cannot, establish the right to have a baby when you want to have a baby. Complete control over reproduction would be a fully symmetric right including a "right to pregnancy" that corresponds to the right to terminate a pregnancy. The Court creates the illusion of far more control over reproduction than is really possible in a process as inherently probabilistic as achieving pregnancy.

Ask a thirty-five year old infertile woman whether she has "the ability to control her reproductive life," and she may just smack you. Her pain is all the more poignant if she has been contracepting for years. Perhaps she did organize her life around the promise of reproductive freedom. But she discovers, too late, that this promise is simply an illusion.

This is why I say that reproductive freedom is empty. It is based on a misunderstanding of the amount of control that is reasonable or desirable in a fully lived human life. We convince ourselves that we are entitled to control the timing and arrival of children. If that is so important to us, isn't it equally important to control who those children are, what those children do, whether those children please us? But this is plainly both impossible and inhumane. Yet that is what we set ourselves up for, when we begin to think in terms of "family planning." It is more realistic to recognize that being sexually active exposes us to a whole host of possibilities, including pregnancy, whose ultimate results we cannot fully anticipate or control. Better to realize that the right to unlimited sexual activity without a live baby resulting is not an entitlement to which we should abandon every other good.

Originally published:
Townhall August 19, 2005

Available on-line at: http://townhall.com/columnists/jenniferrobackmorse/2005/08/19/the_illusions_of_reproductive_freedom_part_i/page/full - Reprinted with permission

SECTION B
A DIFFERENT KIND OF FREEDOM

~ 9 ~

Myths Of Reproductive Freedom:
Part II

REPEALING THE LAW OF CAUSE AND EFFECT

IT IS STARTLING TO realize that the looming battle for the Supreme Court hinges on whether nominees will pledge their support for the utterly irrational demand to suspend the law of cause and effect. For that is what the claim that we have a constitutional right to "reproductive freedom" amounts to. All Americans are entitled to have the cause, namely, unlimited sexual activity, without ever experiencing the effect, namely, a live baby. To see the absurdity of this claim, try out a couple of analogies.

Consider eating, for instance. We can all agree that eating is a good and necessary thing, that everyone is entitled to eat. We might even agree that gourmet eating is one of life's great pleasures. We would not conclude that everyone has a constitutional right to eat as much as they want, without ever getting heart disease, high blood pressure or other natural consequences of overeating. We could not coherently claim that every person has a constitutional right to eat without getting fat, and call it "gastronomical freedom." (Although, considering the number of overweight people in our country, maybe people do think they have such an entitlement.)

Likewise, no one is entitled to eat as little as possible, with a guarantee that they will never succumb to anorexia. You are free to purge yourself after every meal, but you are going to create a whole string of negative consequences for yourself. The state can not reasonably promise to suspend the laws of cause and effect to provide its citizens with the gastronomical self-determination that would allow them to eat or not eat, as much or as little as they want, without any negative consequences.

This is not an ideological argument, because it does not depend on any particular view of the proper role of the state, and the proper scope of its guarantees. Advocates of the welfare state might well argue that everyone has a right to food, at state expense if necessary. It does not logically follow from this that everyone has a right to eat nothing but butter and never get heart disease. Advocates of more minimal government might argue that people have every right to such food as they can obtain through fair market exchanges and gifts. But no libertarian would claim that people have a right to eat without consequences. No legislator in his right mind would attempt to pass a law guaranteeing such a thing. The very idea is reminiscent of a state legislature's notorious attempt to pass a law declaring the value of "pi" to be an even 3, rather than that irrational number with lots of pesky decimal places.

We don't usually think of freedom as the right to suspend the laws of cause and effect in order to obtain what we want. We don't think of freedom of movement as meaning the right to jump off the Golden Gate Bridge and not die. Freedom of assembly doesn't mean an entitlement for an entire fraternity to actually fit inside a telephone booth, however much they might enjoy trying. Freedom of speech can't mean the right to shoot off our mouths any time we want, and still have friends. No court of law could grant such a right.

Nor do sensible people think of freedom as the equivalent of "being in possession of all good things." Central heating and air conditioning are wonderful inventions that have greatly improved people's comfort and well-being. That doesn't mean that being without air conditioning is a deprivation of freedom. It is an inconvenience if the central heat goes out, but it is not the equivalent of slavery. You may regard contraceptive devices as the greatest things since sliced bread. That doesn't mean freedom means using them without failure. You may think that low-cost abortion is on balance, a good thing. That doesn't mean women are slaves if they must bear some costs associated with abortion.

Reproductive freedom is different in kind from the more basic economic and political freedoms. These older freedoms guarantee that people have the opportunity to participate in the economic and political systems under a set of transparent rules that apply to everyone. Political and economic freedoms are not guarantees of getting the particular outcomes we want.

Economic liberty doesn't mean the right to succeed in business, only the right to try. And economic freedom certainly doesn't mean that we are entitled to have the job we want, at the wages we want, whether or not we show up for work. Implicit in the notion of economic freedom is the individual's responsibility to play by the rules of the marketplace.

We don't think of political freedom as the right to have our preferred candidates always win elections, only that they have a right to compete in any election. It simply can't be that I am unfree if my candidate doesn't win, or if my policies are not enacted. Losing an election does not make me unfree.

Legal scholars will argue that the right to privacy upon which *Roe v. Wade* depends exists nowhere in the Constitution. I go one step further: the concept of "reproductive freedom" which *Roe* attempts to establish is incoherent. It truly is irrational to insist that nominees to the Supreme Court pledge their allegiance to the doctrine of abortion on demand.

*Originally published: Townhall
September 6, 2005*

Available on-line at: http://townhall.com/columnists/jenniferrobackmorse/2005/09/06/myths_of_
reproductive_freedom_part_ii_--_repealing_the_law_of_cause_and_effect/page/full - Reprinted
with permission

~ 10 ~

What About Those Octuplets?

The two previous articles were written in 2005. I asserted that "reproductive freedom" was only the right to say "no," to pregnancy, but could not possibly guarantee a positive right to become pregnant. As it turns out, I underestimated the draw of the idea of "a right to have a baby." By 2009, it had become necessary to point out that there is no positive right to have a baby.

WHAT ARE WE TO make of the case of Nadya Suleman, the California woman who gave birth to octuplets through *in vitro* fertilization? The case has inspired lots of internet chatter and water cooler talk. I maintain that insurance and government funding are the least of the worries of this case. The case illustrates two deep problems with our current attitudes toward artificial reproductive technology. First, no one has a right to have a baby. Second, the state should not be in the business of deliberately separating fathers from their children.

No one has a right to a baby. That is because becoming a parent is something no one can do alone. It is the ultimate team effort. To say that a woman is entitled to a baby comes awfully close to saying that someone is required to help her have one. But this is obviously nonsense. No one is required to help her.

What we mean to say when we think that someone has a right to a baby is something like this: I have the right to try to persuade someone to cooperate with me in the physical act necessary to create a baby. I am not entitled to the cooperation of any one particular person, or to some generalized cooperation from society at large. I am only entitled to try.

If I am successful at getting someone's cooperation, the child's father has as much entitlement to that child as I do. Both parents have rights and responsibilities toward their child. This protects the legitimate interests of the child in having the care of both parents, as well as the legitimate interests of both parents in the well-being of their child. Those rights, which flow naturally from the organic reality of human sexuality, inhere in both parents.

Even if one agrees with me that no woman is entitled to the cooperation of any particular man in impregnating her, one might still object that my position is hopelessly old-fashioned and out-of-date. Technology relieves us of the necessity of having any kind of personal relationship with your child's other parent. We allow unmarried women access to artificial reproductive technology, complete with anonymous sperm donors, on a regular, and completely unregulated basis. So why are we now all of a sudden hysterical over a woman exercising her "free choice" to implant all the frozen embryos she has on hand? Any woman is entitled to unlimited access to the use of artificial reproductive technology, provided that she can pay for it.

But look at what this position actually entails. We are permitting women to have babies without any relationship with their child's father. Under normal circumstances, we think there is something wrong with parents who don't cooperate with each other for the good of their children. In the case of artificial reproductive technology, we not only permit it, we enlist the aid of the state to make it possible. The legal intervention of the state permits a woman to do something that could not be possible in the ordinary course of human life: she can have a baby without ever having even a single encounter with her child's father. The state enables all the arrangements that make this possible. The state makes the sperm donor, that is to say, the child's father, a "legal stranger" to the child. The state preserves the anonymity of the donor, which obviously could not happen in a normal encounter.

Now children get separated from their parents all the time. But we usually recognize this as an unavoidable tragedy, from which any humane soul would spare the child if we could. But in the case of artificial reproductive technology with anonymous sperm donors, the state is actively separating a child from his or her father. The state itself is enabling something that we ordinarily strive to prevent.

And why is the state acting as the agent of separating children from parents? Because the woman wants the state to do so. But her desires are not a sufficient reason to violate so basic a right as the child's right to affiliation with both parents.

This is the real tragedy which the Nadya Suleman case brings to light. It is not that she made an unconventional decision, in part using other people's money, and counting on financial support from her parents and the state. The problem is that no one has a right to have a child, in the way that anyone with the ability to pay has a right to buy a house. This use of the language of the market assumes the very point that is necessary to prove, and which I believe can not be proved: namely that a child is a kind of commodity, to which other people have rights and entitlements. The child is not an object of rights, but a person who has rights of his or her own. The child is an end in himself or herself.

The violation of rights in this case took place well before she and her doctor decided to implant "a lot" of embryos, rather than a "reasonable" number. The real violation took place when she decided, with the help of the state, that she was entitled to the use of someone else's genetic material to achieve her personal reproductive goals.

I am second to none in my admiration for the market. But not everything should be treated as if it were a commodity. Children are not commodities, and neither is someone else's genetic material. It is time to rethink our whole approach to artificial reproductive technology.

Originally published: MercatorNet.com
March 6, 2009

Available on-line at: http://www.mercatornet.com/articles/view/what_about_those_
octuplets#sthash.xWGhaUK8.dpuf - Reprinted with permission

SECTION C
CONTRACEPTION
AND
ABORTION

~ 11 ~

If Only We Had Enough Condoms

CONTRACEPTION HAS ALWAYS BEEN part of a package sold in the name of health, wealth and saving the world. The twentieth century witnessed so much bloodshed in the name of ideology you might think people would be ready to give it a rest. But no, we have a new ideology whose adherents believe will usher in a new heaven on earth. If only everyone would finally get on board, if only its adherents had the right combination of money and power, if only its Neanderthal opponents would surrender their squeamishness, this new ideology could solve the world's problems. Poverty, environmental degradation and disease would be conquered at last. The name of this new ideology? I call it "condom-ism."

Its adherents believe we could solve all these problems, if only we had enough condoms. I exaggerate, of course. They actually believe that human salvation will require all sorts of birth control including abortion, not just condoms.

A recent edition of the widely-read British medical journal, *The Lancet,* spells out some of the tenets of this position. The authors opine that "family planning" still matters because population growth retards economic growth, or exacerbates poverty. They themselves admit that the economic evidence for their position is slim, because "poverty reduction is also affected by many other forces."[1] Good point. Last I looked, the West developed economically sometime in the 18th century. That was before the Pill, wasn't it? Gosh, maybe transparent government, rule of law, property rights and stable currency have more to do with poverty reduction than condoms.

Lower population growth is good, we are told, because it "provides countries with a unique, but transient opportunity to make rapid gains in living standards, because income can be used for productive investment rather than expended on support of young and old people."[2] Funny, I thought supporting the young was

---

1 "Family planning: the unfinished agenda," John Cleland, et.al. published on-line, November 1, 2006 at http://dx.doi.org/10.1016/S0140-6736(06)69480-4. Print edition: Volume 368, No. 9549, p1810–1827, 18 November 2006.
2 *Ibid.*, Panel 4.

a productive investment and helping the old a duty of civilized people. No word from our authors about how countries with declining fertility rates, like Japan, Russia and Korea, are going to take care of the increasing number of dependent elderly people.

Environmental sustainability? Everyone knows that large populations are the scourge of the earth. But even our authors admit that richer countries take better care of the environment than do desperately poor countries. Never mind. More condoms will save the earth.

We don't have to view contraception through this ideological lens. It is theoretically possible that contraception could simply be a morally neutral technology, which people could use to change the probability of any given sexual act resulting in pregnancy. While this is possible in principle, in fact, contraception in America has never been merely a technology.

Nor do its proponents view it as simply an option for the Third World. The authors lament the fact that many women, particularly in Africa, want large families, and that many people discontinue the use of contraceptives — at a rate of 12 percent for the IUD and 47 percent for the condom.[3] These people are not ignorant or ill-informed; they quit using contraception because they want to.

Giving people choices has never been enough for the radical advocates of condom-ism. Contraception has always been part of an ideological package. Here are some of its major tenets:

» Every person capable of giving meaningful consent is entitled to unlimited sexual activity.

» All negative consequences of sexual activity can be controlled or eliminated through the use of contraception. Sexually transmitted diseases can be controlled through the use of condoms. The probability of pregnancy can be eliminated through contraception, properly used.

» No one is required to give birth to a baby, in the event of pregnancy. Abortion, for any reason or no reason, at any time during pregnancy, is an absolute entitlement.

» Any negative consequences of sexual activity that cannot be handled by contraception or abortion are not worth talking about. No one ever gets attached to a sex partner who turns out to be inappropriate. No one ever regrets a consensual sexual experience. The evidence linking teen sex to depres-

---

3   *Ibid.*, Section entitled "Family Planning Methods," Table 3. Note the high discontinuance rates of the "LARCs:" Long-Acting Reversible Contraceptives, such as Implants and Injectables.

sion must be dismissed or discredited. Adultery and the disruption of an established family? Not to worry: follow your bliss.

And don't forget, we could save the earth, end world hunger and bring peace and freedom to the entire world, if only we had enough condoms.

Many traditional societies resist this ideological tied-sale. Even if some of them would like contraception to be available, they don't want to buy the whole Playboy, MTV bundle that seems to be attached to it. We in the developed world have no business foisting this cultural package onto our poorer neighbors.

Originally published: Mercatornet.com
November 24, 2006

Available on-line at http://www.mercatornet.com/articles/view/focus_on_reproductive_health_if_only_we_had_enough_condoms - Reprinted with permission

~ 12 ~

Plan B Is a Bad Plan

ITH BAD NEWS TO come.

The dispute over the morning-after pill has hinged on the politics of FDA approval and the science of abortion. Did the FDA withhold approval just to placate Bush's conservative base? Is Plan B really "emergency contraception" or it is really a very early abortion? Now that the morning-after pill has been approved for over-the-counter use, we need to ask ourselves how it will affect the spread of Sexually Transmitted Diseases (STDs). I predict the morning-after pill will induce a new round of increases in sexually transmitted diseases.

I base my opinion on the dynamics of contraceptive failure. We know that contraceptive failure is a function of age, income, and marital status. Younger women, unmarried women, and poor women are more likely to experience a contraceptive failure. Consider the rate of contraceptive failure for oral contraceptives, widely considered the most reliable of all the reversible, non-long-acting contraceptive methods. The failure rate of the Pill is 13 percent for poor married women under the age of 20, and declines to just under half that rate to 5.7 percent, for married poor women over 30. The age-specific failure rate is even more dramatic for cohabiting, but not married couples: For poor cohabiting women under age 20, the failure rate of the pill is 48 percent, while for poor cohabiting women over age 30, the failure rate is a mere 10.8 percent.

The failure rates for condom use are similarly correlated with age, income and marital status. The most successful users of condoms are married women over age 30 who are not poor. Of women in this group whose primary birth-control method is condoms, 6 percent can expect to be pregnant within a year. By contrast, among unmarried poor women under age 20, 23 percent will be pregnant within a year. The most spectacular failure rates are for cohabiting, poor women under the age of 20: 72 percent of them who use condoms as their regular birth control method will be pregnant within a year's time.

What is going on here? Obviously, the pills don't know the woman's age or income. The condoms aren't surreptitiously trying to enforce "family values," by breaking more often for women "living in sin" than for married women. The pills are "failing" because the women aren't taking them. The condoms are "failing" because people aren't using them regularly. The failure rate in this study is measured as the percentage of women, using a regular method of birth control, who become pregnant within a year's time. Married women, more mature women, and higher-income women are more likely to take their pills regularly and use condoms consistently. The high failure rates for cohabiting women occur because cohabiting women have more sex than other unmarried women.

What does this tell us about the likely impact of the wide availability of the morning-after pill? For those women who rely on birth-control pills for contraception, MAP will probably not change their behavior. If they are taking the pills but not regularly, they presumably still believe they are protected. They are not likely to get up the next morning and run to the drug store.

But for people who are using condoms but not reliably, the morning-after pill will become not Plan B, but Plan A, the birth-control method of first choice. "Oh honey, stop, we've got to put on a condom." "Don't worry, baby. I'll get you the pills tomorrow."

Even with all the publicity and education surrounding "safe sex," not everyone at risk for STDs uses a condom every time. Pausing to put on a condom interrupts the flow and spontaneity of the sexual act. Persuading people to do that consistently is a tough sell. It's even a tougher sell to people who already have another birth-control method, like the Pill. With the advent of Plan B, everyone has a method other than condoms. If you think preaching abstinence is unrealistic, try preaching consistent condom use to people who already have a foolproof birth-control method.

I predict an increase in sexual activity, unprotected by condoms. I also wouldn't be surprised to see an increase in sexual activity overall, as people believe themselves to be "safe" from pregnancy, due to the availability of the morning-after pill as emergency contraception.

But being "safe" from pregnancy isn't the same as being "safe" from STDs. Look for an increased rate of STD infections over the next few years.

You heard it here first.

Note to reader: In 2006, when this article was written, the number of cases of Syphilis in the United States was 36,958. By 2013, the most recent year data is available, the number of cases was 56,471. For Chlamydia, there were 1,030,911 cases in the United States in 2006. By 2013, there were 1,401,906. The cases of gonorrhea dipped slightly from 2006 to 2010, but then began to rise again, according to the study by the CDC found here: http://www.cdc.gov/std/stats13/tables/1.htm.

Originally published: National Review Online
September 14, 2006

http://www.nationalreview.com/articles/218715/plan-b-bad-plan/jennifer-roback-morse - Reprinted with permission

Contraceptive failure rates quoted in this article, can be found at: "Contraceptive Failure Rates in the US: New Estimates from the 1995 National Survey of Family Growth," by Haishan Fu, Jacqueline E. Darroch, Taylor Haas and Nalini Ranjit, Family Planning Perspectives, Vol. 31, No. 2, 1999.

Available on-line at http://www.guttmacher.org/pubs/journals/3105699.html

~ 13 ~

The Pill: Past Its Use-by Date

HOW QUICKLY THINGS CAN change. One week we read about the need for school nurses to give contraceptive pills to girls who just can't say no; the next, this headline from London's Daily Telegraph leaps out from our news feeds: "'Contraceptive pill outdated and does not work well,' experts warns".

Well, I thought, that is curious. Whatever could have happened? Are women all of a sudden immune to the effects of estrogen? Is it something in the air, or the water? And who was the expert delivering this disturbing news?

It turned out to be Dr. James Trussell, Professor of Economics and Public Affairs and Director of the Office of Population Research at Princeton University. Dr. Trussell is one of the Mr. Bigs of birth control research so the Telegraph was listening carefully when he spoke recently at a conference of one of the UK's main birth control groups, the British Pregnancy Advisory Service.

And yes, he certainly was disenchanted with the Pill. "One in 12 women taking the Pill get pregnant each year because they miss so many tablets," he lamented. "The Pill is an outdated method because it does not work well enough. It is very difficult for ordinary women to take a pill every single day."

Frankly, this is something well known in Britain where pregnancy rates among schoolgirls continue to rise, and thousands of women have three or four abortions. But what does Dr. Trussell suggest should be done with these "ordinary women" who, although he is too polite to say it in so many words, are too stupid to take a pill every day?

Shoot them up with long-lasting hormonal contraception amounting to sterilization — not to put too fine a point on it. "The beauty of the implant or the IUD is that you can forget about them," enthused the professor. "If you want to seriously reduce unintended pregnancies in the UK you can only do it with implants and IUDs."

So now we get to the heart of the matter. The problem is not that the Pill doesn't work — it does, reducing the probability that any given act of intercourse will result in pregnancy. The problem is that women do not take it regularly enough. But that raises the all-important question: What, exactly, are we trying to accomplish with the Pill?

This is my theory: the Pill has been an instrument in the creation of what author Lee Harris called, in another context, a fantasy ideology.

A fantasy ideology is a variety of utopianism that is not about making a better world, but making its adherents feel good about themselves. The believer is assured that he is one of the chosen, one of the few enlightened ones who truly understands the universe. In the name of supporting the fantasy, the believer is entitled to impose large costs on other people. Indeed, he seldom notices these costs, because he is not checking in with reality on a regular basis. Data fly right over his head.

Though Lee Harris developed his concept of the fantasy ideology in relation to Islam, his analysis could apply just as well to the contraceptive ideology. The fantasy ideology of contraception is that people are entitled to behave as if they had perfectly functioning contraception; in other words, to act as though sexual activity and reproduction are completely disconnected.

Adherents of the ideology get to feel good about themselves as progressive, modern, enlightened. They are ever so beyond the tired old ethics that connects sex with responsible parenthood through marriage. Most importantly, believers in the faith that contraception prevents all consequences of sex never have to apologize for any sexual misdeeds. There are no sexual misdeeds, with the possible exception of rape.

It is no wonder that poor Dr. Trussell is disappointed. The Pill could not possibly meet the standard of creating a lifetime of harmless and guilt-free sex.

Yet on the road to the society of perfectly controlled reproductive freedom, millions of people's lives have been ruined. Women got themselves involved in relationships that had no chance of sustaining a pregnancy. Then, they were shocked and appalled when they got pregnant. In their desperation, they turned to abortion. Or they kept babies they were ill-prepared to raise, because they could not bring themselves to have an abortion and no-one encouraged them to consider adoption.

Or, men got themselves involved with women who claimed they wanted no deeper involvement. But then, when they became pregnant, they wanted the child after all. In some cases the woman wanted the child all along, and deceived the man into believing that he was participating in a sterile sexual encounter. Since sterile sex is the new social norm, thanks to the Pill, it is not difficult to convince a man you don't mean to have a baby.

Men and women alike thought the addition of a condom protected them from sexually transmitted diseases. They didn't notice when the sexual spin doctors quietly changed the term "safe sex" to "safer sex". Some were naïve enough to think that the Pill looked after all safety issues, even though it offers no protection against STDs whatsoever.

The true believer in the fantasy ideology of contraception does not look too closely at problems like these. Any problem that cannot be solved by more contraception is not worth considering.

This is why the indefatigable Dr. Trussell advocates more aggressive and intrusive methods of contraception. He and his allies must not, at any cost, question their premise that contraception eliminates all negative consequences of sex. They are reduced to sewing more patches over the tattered quilt of an outmoded fantasy ideology. It is not just the Pill that has outlived its shelf life, but the contraceptive ideology itself.

Originally published: Mercatornet.com
July 31, 2008

Available on-line at: http://www.mercatornet.com/articles/view/the_pill_past_its_use_by_date - Reprinted with permission

Addition to Article 13: "The Pill: Past its Use-By Date," "'Contraceptive Pill outdated and does not work well,' expert warns," Daily Telegraph, June 25, 2008. Available on-line at: http://www.telegraph.co.uk/news/uknews/2193112/Contraceptive-Pill-is-outdated-and-does-not-work-well-expert-warns.html

~ 14 ~

Excuse Me, Madam Speaker

If Nancy Pelosi wants to save the American economy some money she needs to stop investing in irresponsible sex.

NANCY PELOSI MADE "STUPID" history this week by her claim that "family planning" funds will stimulate the economy. Her argument, if you can dignify it with that term, is that reducing unwanted pregnancies will reduce the burden on tax-payers. But she doesn't ask herself whether more contraception is really the answer to "unwanted" pregnancies.

I recently had the opportunity to visit with some teen mothers in Reno, Nevada. Casa de Vida is a private, nonprofit corporation providing a home and support services for pregnant young women. The youngest was 14; the oldest was just 20. These are, presumably, the mothers whose pregnancies are expensive to the taxpayers. These young unmarried mothers need a variety of social services in order to take care of their babies. The Casa has a special classroom set up in their basement, so the girls can finish high school. Some will be unable to go back to their families for a variety of reasons and will need subsidized housing. Many take advantage of jobs training programs. And, of course, virtually none of them have their own health insurance, so the taxpayers pay for medical care for the mothers and babies. The social worker refers them to the public services for which they qualify.

I came at the invitation of some of the board members to talk with the girls about sex. Their social worker wanted me to help them think about having a plan for dealing with the desires they are sure to have for another relationship with a man. Neither I nor the social worker had any illusion that one chat in an afternoon will change the whole course of their lives. But we do hope that we gave them a few thoughts that will lodge in their brains when they need them later.

So we talked about their hopes and dreams for their babies. These young women want to be good mothers, and they want to be loved. Right now, they are focused on the immediate fact that their babies will be born soon. I tried to help them think about their futures beyond the birth of their babies. One day, they will be interested in boys again. Their social worker had told me that

71

a) most of them won't even consider adoption and b) most of them will be pregnant again within two years.

Talking with them helped me to see why the whole contraception approach to avoiding teen pregnancy is so hopeless. These girls get pregnant because they want to: they want to be loved by their boyfriends, and by their babies. Contraception is notoriously unreliable among teens. Even among women seeking abortions, who you might think would be especially motivated to avoid pregnancy, 53 percent were using some form of contraception at the time they conceived.[1] Passing out pills or promising abortions doesn't deal with the underlying desires that are driving their behavior.

Social worker Paula Crandall and Casa de Vida board member Kathleen Rossi told me that, sometimes, the Casa turns out to be the best thing that ever happened to the girls. Some of them are able to develop a sense of their own worth as persons. They get adult assistance in the ordinary problems of living, such as finishing high school, applying for jobs, looking for an apartment and so on. For some of them, the staff members at the Casa are the first adults who have taken a real interest in them, and who have the means to really help them with these basic skills. No amount of "comprehensive sex education" or "access to reproductive health" can meet these very deep-seated human needs.

If Nancy Pelosi wants to reduce the costs to taxpayers, she should be promoting marriage. Out-of-wedlock childbearing is one of the surest roads to poverty and, thereby, to taxpayer expenditure. A recent study by the Institute for American Values conservatively estimated the taxpayer costs of non-marital childbearing to be $112 billion per year, or roughly the GDP of New Zealand. Responsible, sustainable childbearing takes place within marriage. And, incidentally, if Speaker Pelosi really wants to reduce abortions (which she hinted at, but did not say) she should also be promoting marriage. Some 80 percent of abortions, year in and year out, are performed on unmarried women.

Having babies and raising them to responsible adulthood is a significant social investment. If the family around the child breaks down or never forms in the first place, the odds of the child be-

---

1   "Contraceptive Use Among U.S. Women Having Abortions in 2000-2001"
     Rachel K. Jones, Jacqueline E. Darroch and Stanley K. Henshaw,
     Perspectives on Sexual and Reproductive Health, Volume 34, Number 6,
     November/December 2002 Available on-line at http://www.guttmacher.org/
     pubs/journals/3429402.html

ing raised to responsible adulthood are greatly reduced. These young girls are having babies not because their contraception has failed, not because they don't know how to use contraception; they are having babies because they want to be loved. If Nancy Pelosi wants to save the taxpayer some money in the long run, she needs to stop investing in irresponsible sex, and start investing in responsible adult supervision and guidance of the young.

I'm not holding my breath.

Originally published: Mercatornet.com
January 30, 2009

Available on-line at: http://www.mercatornet.com/articles/view/excuse_me_madam_
speaker#sthash.HKORI8UP.dpuf - Reprinted with permission

~ 15 ~

The New Contraceptive Order Can Only Kill Itself

THE 50TH ANNIVERSARY OF the birth control pill — the Food and Drug Administration gave it final approval in 1960 — has been the occasion of much media fanfare, societal reflection — and what we might call Secular Triumphalism. We, the Enlightened, knew all along that giving women control over their fertility was going to be simply marvelous. End of story. Some of us have tried to point out that the pill had some negative consequences, but few seem interested.

The reason for the disconnect is that the ideology surrounding the pill is more significant than the pill itself.

Behind the apparently benign goal of giving people more choices lies a deeper goal: re-creating society. And since this new society is neither appealing nor natural, its advocates are not so eager to call attention to it.

The New Contraceptive World Order holds these tenets: Sex is a sterile recreational activity. "Safe" sex (meaning sex with a condom) has no significant negative consequences. Marriage is not necessary for either sexual activity or childbearing. And unlimited sexual activity is an entitlement for everyone old enough to give meaningful consent.

But there is a serpent in this man-made paradise: All of these tenets are false.

It isn't true that sex is a sterile activity. Contraception fails — regularly. Even the pill only reduces the probability of pregnancy, but not all the way to zero. Uncommitted sex has plenty of negative consequences that cannot be prevented by contraception. Marriage really is the best place for both sexual activity and childbearing. And, because we have been convinced that unlimited sexual activity is an entitlement, we have sex in relationships that cannot possibly sustain a pregnancy. When the inevitable pregnancies result, we fall back on abortion to continue clinging to our belief in the New Contraceptive World Order.

Thus, the attempt to create this new society cannot succeed.

The New Contraceptive World Order is an artificial creation of

75

the state. It requires continual support and coddling from the state, including ever-increasing efforts to suppress dissent and enforce conformity.

Cheerleaders for this new heaven on earth insist that all doctors be trained in abortions, that all pharmacists prescribe all forms of birth control, that all employers provide contraception and abortion in their health plans. Suppressing the choices of doctors, pharmacists, insurers and employers makes no sense — unless the real goal is to create the new and unnatural society of sterile sex.

Public-interest law firms defending First Amendment rights report that student pro-life groups are subjected to more restrictions on their free-speech rights than virtually any other student groups.

Obviously, restricting free speech in the name of reproductive "freedom" is incoherent. None of this would be necessary if the only purpose of the pill were to give everyone more choices.

This fundamental incoherence is also the underlying cause of the contentiousness of the Supreme Court nomination process. Since this new world cannot sustain itself by the ordinary actions of ordinary people making voluntary decisions, it has to be sustained by the continual applications of force by those in power. This explains why the stakes for seats in the judiciary are so high.

You might think that consistent failures would compel people to reconsider their ideas about sex. But this cannot be left to chance. The propaganda surrounding the pill has been just as revolutionary as the pill itself. Griswold v. Connecticut, allowing married couples to access contraception to reduce the probability of pregnancy, was never enough for the radicals of the sexual revolution.

To bring their dream world into existence, contraception has to be actively promoted. The federal government finances contraception education in public schools. The sexual-revolution radicals become hysterical over the mere mention of abstinence education. Even people who are normally not ideological have become convinced that it is more "realistic" to expect teenagers to use a condom every time than to persuade them to postpone sexual activity in the first place.

As for the great benefits to women supposedly created by contraception, consider this: In the New Contraceptive World Order, women have the freedom to participate in the labor market on the same terms as men with this proviso: We agree to

76

chemically neuter ourselves during our peak reproductive years.

But it never was necessary for women to make the Faustian bargain. The trend toward the increasing participation of women in higher education and the labor force began around the turn of the 20th century — well before the pill, *The Feminine Mystique* and the National Abortion Rights Action League (NARAL). Women never needed contraception to be free, even according to the crabbed and truncated vision of freedom that claims that acting on impulse is the ultimate expression of human liberty.

The Catholic Church and other advocates of natural society have taken a beating for being hopelessly "out of step" with modern times.

Do not be deceived by this incessant rhetoric.

The New Contraceptive World Order is inhuman, irrational and, ultimately, unsustainable. It is time to insist that our government stop trying to create something that would not make us happy — even if it could be forced into being, which it cannot.

© National Catholic Register

Originally published: NCRegister.com
June 28, 2010

Available on-line at: http://www.ncregister.com/site/article/the_new_contraceptive_order_can_

only_kill_itself/ - Reprinted with permission

~ 16 ~

How the Pro-Choice Movement Scared America

A BOOK WITH A PRESUMPTUOUS title like, *How the Pro-Choice Movement Saved America: Freedom, Politics and the War on Sex,* had better deliver. Cristina Page's book of this title tries to motivate people by scaring them. Pro-life advocates will not recognize themselves in the cartoon caricature Ms. Page presents of them. The vast numbers of middle of the road Americans, to whom this book is presumably addressed, won't respond to it either. But there is one thing Page does get right: America is engaged in a titanic struggle over the meaning of sex.

Her version of how the pro-choice movement saved America? If it weren't for NARAL, Pro-Choice America, women would be home baking cookies for children and would never have made it into the work place. Never mind that the trend toward increasing labor force participation of married women goes all the way back to the turn of the twentieth century. If it weren't for the pro-choice movement, abortion and contraception would be illegal in all states. Never mind that both abortion and contraception were legal in some states well before the Supreme Court decisions that discovered constitutional privacy rights to these things. If *Roe v. Wade* is overturned, women will be reduced to trying to end their own pregnancies by having their boyfriends whack their bellies with a baseball bat. She never mentions the women who have died from legal abortions in this country.

Page criticizes crisis pregnancy centers, which pro-life groups have established all across America, because they don't give "accurate information." The thousands of pro-life women who have donated millions of dollars worth of free medical care, baby clothes and supplies, and countless volunteer hours, will not recognize themselves in her description. In fact, I doubt that she grasps the significance of the term "pro-life women," since she barely seems to acknowledge their existence.

But let's not quibble with Ms. Page about the caricature she presents of the pro-life movement. Let's cut to the chase and address the question. What is sex all about?

Unlike Ms. Page, I am not going to try to pin the blame for the current condition of our sexual culture on any one group. Feminists, pornographers and certain parts of our corporate culture share some responsibility, along with abortion rights advocacy groups. But I do think groups like NARAL, Cristina Page's employer, have a serious responsibility for the current condition of our culture.

The modern view holds that sex is a recreational activity with no moral or social significance. The freedom we have come to value is to be completely unencumbered by human relationships. We are entitled to end or walk away from any relationship with a person who might legitimately make demands upon us that we don't want to fulfill. And reproductive freedom in particular, is the right to unlimited sexual activity without a live baby resulting.

I call this view of sex, Consumer Sex. The decision to have sex is comparable to the decision to go bowling or go out for pizza. If sex is a recreational activity, that makes our sex partners consumer goods, that satisfy us more or less well. And when we are no longer satisfied with our sex partners, we feel entitled to discard them. We believe it is morally acceptable to use another person, as long as they consent to being used. As long as the sex was voluntary and properly contracepted, it is OK. I need not say that this attitude toward sex would be impossible in the absence of abortion on demand and unlimited access to contraception.

The alternative view is the organic view of human sexuality. Sex has two organic purposes: procreation and spousal unity. Spousal unity is a fancy way of saying that sex builds up the relationship between the husband and the wife. Unbeknownst to critics like Cristina Page, the Christian view of sexuality has recognized spousal unity as a legitimate purpose of sex since the Middle Ages. Both of these organic purposes build up the community of the family. Procreation brings new people into being. And spousal unity helps to sustain the bond between the spouses, so they will be there for each other and their children over the long-haul.

Consumer Sex turns this organic reality on its head. Consumer Sex takes the sexual urge, which is a great engine of sociability, and turns into a consumer good. Instead of seeing sex as something that builds up the family and the community, we see sex as something that is all about me and my feelings.

Cristina Page and her companions believe they are promoting the view that sex is for pleasure. But who takes pleasure in being used? The sexual revolution, of which NARAL is so proud, has not made people happy. This is the primary reason why not: no matter how much fun we're having while we are using another person, we don't want to be on the receiving end of being used.

Adopting the label of "pro-choice" obscures the subject of the choice. When you spell out the pro-choice position, it is not really all that appealing. In my own book, *Smart Sex: Finding Lifelong Love in a Hook-up World,* I say nothing about what should be legal or illegal. I simply point out that many of our (perfectly legal) sexual decisions are just plain dumb.

I challenge Cristina Page to a debate. I will debate her on the airwaves. I will debate her in person. I'll debate her on her own terms, in the style of the Yale Political Union: "Resolved: that contraception is the greatest thing since sliced bread." Then we will find out who is saving America and who is just trying to scare it to death.

*Originally published: Townhall.com
April 17, 2006*

Available on-line at: http://townhall.com/columnists/jenniferrobackmorse/2006/04/17/how_the_
pro-choice_movement_scared_america/page/full - Reprinted with permission

Note: this is the article which prompted the debate I alluded to in the first article of this book.

SECTION D
THE PROBLEMS
OF THE
CAREER WOMAN

~ 17 ~

Beyond "Having It All"

*Note: This was originally a talk delivered at a Federalist Society
Conference at the University of Virginia, in 1994.*

THE TITLE OF THIS panel is "Rational Choices." We are to
consider the proposition that women are less well off than
men because they rationally choose different life goals, and
rationally pursue different strategies for achieving those goals.
The starting point for the discussion is the observation that
women earn less money than men, with income equality as the
implicit touch-stone for the desirability of policies, personal or
public. Indeed, the goal of income equality is so widely accepted
that even the organizers of this panel, hardly radical feminists,
assumed its validity.

Of course, defining one's well-being in terms of one's income is
not self-evidently correct. In fact, it is extremely problematic to
argue that one's income is an accurate measure of one's wealth,
even on strictly economic grounds. The overall claim is even more
problematic if we consider, as we ought, the questions of "What is
the good life?" or "What is the life well-lived?" — the philosophi-
cal questions that have engaged the attention and efforts of the
deepest and most thoughtful of us since time immemorial. Indeed, it is only in the late twentieth century, when people have
become obsessed with money, that anyone would even consider
the question of rationality in terms of one's success in earning
and accumulating money.

In this paper, I want to move the topic of rationality into a somewhat different arena. Is the strategy of the women's movement a
rational choice for improving the well-being of women, defined by
these broader criteria? And if not, what alternatives do we have?

I want to present some alternative visions.

THE ISSUES WOMEN FACE

The women's movement has tried to deal with two different but
related trends: first, the entry of married women into the labor
force, and second, the insecurity of women within marriages.
The trend toward increased labor force participation pre-dates

85

the women's movement, as ordinarily defined.[1] The increase in the labor force participation of married women dates from the beginning of the twentieth century.[2] The increase in the level of divorces can be observed as early as 1970.[3]

These two trends may be related in the following way: because of the increased probability of divorce, women rationally chose to commit themselves more fully to labor market participation than they otherwise would have. If women can no longer look forward to financial security within marriage, a rational response certainly might be to plan for financial independence.[4] According to this view, the increase in the divorce rate is a cause of increased labor force participation rather than the other way around. To use the language of Carol Rose's provocative article, a rational strategy for women would be to pursue credible alternatives to staying within a relationship which may prove exploitive.[5]

At the same time, an increase in a woman's financial security might lead her to be less committed to her marriage. Whatever other benefits she may receive from her married life, a woman with the human capital to support herself financially needs her husband less than she otherwise would. This effect has been noted and described as the "disposable man" or "disposable father" syndrome.[6]

Of course, there is much more that could be said about the relationship between the demographic trends of increased labor force activity and increased marital instability. Many within the women's movement have said a great deal about how women ought to deal with these two issues. How should we behave inside the labor force, and what should our goals there be? How should we interact with our husbands; indeed, what kinds of husbands should we seek? It will not be possible to do full justice to these important topics. I will address one of the strategies

1   We might date the beginning of the women's movement from the publication of Betty Friedan, **The Feminine Mystique** (1963)
2   Claudia Goldin, Understanding the Gender Gap: an Economic History of American Women; (Oxford: **Oxford University Press,** 1992) 16-17, Table 2.1
3   The divorce rate per thousand population in 1965 was 2.5; by 1970 it had risen to 3.5. **Statistical Abstract of the United States**, Table 126 (110th ed. 1990)
4   See F. Carolyn Graglia, "The Housewife as Pariah," **18 Harv. J.L. & Pub. Pol'y 509** (1995)
5   Carol M. Rose, "Women and Property: Gaining Ground and Losing Ground," 78 VA. L. REV. 421, 454-55 (1992)
6   *Cf.* Ellen Goodman, "The New Fatherless," **The Washington Post,** June 14, 1983 AT A19

that has been suggested to women of my generation. I will show how it bears upon both of the issues I have outlined, and why I think the strategy is flawed. I will then present two alternative strategies for consideration.

THE MYTH OF HAVING IT ALL

Consider the slogan that was for many of us, both a personal goal, and a political rallying-cry: "Having It All." When stated as a goal, the idea of "having it all" is frankly impossible. This goal assumes that women do not have to face constraints, that there are no choices that exclude other choices. In economic jargon, this objective assumes that women have no budget constraints and face no opportunity costs.

But plainly, women, like men, must make choices. No one can "have it all." The attempt to achieve this objective has made frazzled wrecks out of many women. We scurry from home to work to the day care center and back home, wondering why there is never enough time to do everything, why we are always exhausted, why we are always snapping at someone, and why our lives lack contentment and serenity. The fact is, we are frazzled because we are not facing the reality of our own finiteness. We refuse to accept the fact that making meaningful choices involves exclusion of other options. We have adopted an ideology that requires us to be perpetually overcommitted.

"But men get to have it all," some women might respond. "Why don't men have to choose between family and career?" We arouse ourselves into a self-righteous anger as we pose these rhetorical questions. Thus, "having it all" was for many of us a political agenda as well as a personal goal. As we have convinced ourselves that we should not have to face choices, that we should be able to have everything we want, we have looked around for someone to blame when the inevitable reality sets in. Usually, we blame a man, or men generally. "If only my husband would do more around the house, if only the government would subsidize child care, if only men were not prejudiced against me, then I could have it all."

The fact is that men do have to face choices as well. A man who chooses to dedicate himself to his career may be married and may father children, but if he spends eighty hours a week at work, he has a family only in the most perfunctory sense. Anyone who believes that it is costless for a man to make his job the most important priority in his life is very much mistaken. The proposition that this choice is costless is only valid in a world in which the only objectives are money, status and power. Such a conclusion would be unthinkable in a sane, human world.

As an aside, let me take note of the fact that many law students will be offered jobs that will require them to spend eighty hours a week in the office. It is perfectly obvious that such a job is a choice that excludes other choices. In particular, one cannot build a lasting, loving relationship with another person in the time left over from an eighty-hour-a-week job. The only thing one would be able to do is use another person. It is a serious wrong to use another person.[7] Despite this simple counsel from common sense morality, we might nevertheless convince ourselves that we are entitled to have a relationship, even when we are unwilling to devote any time to learn about, care for, and give to the other person.

If we enter into married life with this thought, we will create a disaster for ourselves, for we will seek out partners who will allow us to use them. Perhaps we will choose someone without enough strength of character to protest being used. Perhaps we will choose someone as ambitious as ourselves, so that they do not object to being used. In short, we will tend to choose someone who will not bother us too much, so that we can devote ourselves to what are plainly our highest priorities, namely, our jobs.

When the marriage dissolves, we have no right to be shocked. The marriage did not end; there was never a marriage there in the first place. The relationship dissolves when that truth can be evaded no longer. Some law students will choose these all-encompassing jobs. I would advise those who are not already in solidly committed relationships, to remain celibate. It does not matter whether one is male or female, an eighty-hour-a-week job is a choice that excludes many other choices.

ALTERNATIVE VISIONS

The Aristotelian Vision

If "Having it All" does not help us to make sense out of our new experiences in the labor market, what might be more helpful? I offer "Live a Balanced Life" as one possibility. This slogan has several virtues. First, it captures what is probably the best intent of the desire to "have it all." Second, it is a slogan that can be applied to men as readily as to women. And finally, living a balanced life is

---

7   See Karol Wojtyla (Pope John Paul, II), **Love and Responsibility** 21-30 (1995, originally published in 1960) Pope John Paul II develops the "personalistic norm" around the proposition that a person may not be an object for use.

a goal that actually can be attained. It calls attention to the fact that we are finite and that we must make choices. It invites us to make our choices thoughtfully. Moreover, our success at living a balanced life is something that only we can judge. It is, by its nature, an objective that focuses on the interior life, not simply on the visible externals.

"Having it all," in practice, means having a career, a marriage, and children. These are readily observable by other people. I think that all too often, women judge themselves and others by the "Super-Mom" criterion. Many women of my generation have suffered unnecessarily from these judgments. Some women have come to feel inadequate because they choose full-time motherhood.[8] And other women feel inadequate because they are unable to do the impossible tasks they have assigned themselves.[9]

Living a balanced life is not something that another person can observe. Others can tell well enough if someone is way off the mark: someone like the eighty-hour-a-week lawyer, for instance, clearly fails any reasonable balance test. For the most part, this is an entirely interior judgment, and in my opinion, that is a good thing. For ultimately, it is not anyone else's place to determine whether another person is a success or a failure.

Had women pursued this strategy, the women's movement would have had an Aristotelian ring to it, as men and women together tried to steer a moderate course through life. We could view the different tendencies among men and women as opportunities for us to moderate each other's excesses. Men could encourage the women in their lives to be more aggressive with respect to the outside world when that would be appropriate or necessary for their best interests. Women can remind the men in their lives that winning is not everything, that the life of the home and the heart is precious and to be cherished, and that they need to admit their mistakes and their weaknesses from time to time in the interest of maintaining friendships and intimacy.

The Aristotelian vision of the ideal marriage is a friendship.[10] The modern notion of spousal equality suggests that justice should be the guiding principle within the marriage. But Aristotle reminds

---

8   Others have resisted these feelings. See, e.g., Graglia, supra note 4
9   See Orania Papazoglou, "Despising Our Mothers, Despising Ourselves," **First Things,** Jan 1992, at 11, 11-19
10   See James V. Schall, "Aristotle on Friendship," 65 **Classical Bulletin** 86 (1969)

us that a friendship has more than "justice" within it. And we might add, that a true marriage needs more than justice. A marriage, like a friendship, is more than a contract.[11]

The Judeo-Christian Vision

Another alternative vision is: "Love Your Neighbor as Yourself."[12] This too, has much to recommend. First of all, loving your neighbor as yourself requires a healthy self-esteem. At the same time, we are invited to moderate this necessary self-esteem, because our attention is immediately directed to the fact that we are not the only persons in the universe. It is a self-esteem that is directed outside ourselves. It is a self-esteem that is not self-centered.

Like living a balanced life, loving one's neighbor as one's self is a program that can be applied as readily to men as it is to women. What kind of world would we be living in, what kind of marriages would we have, if our husbands loved us as they love themselves? What kind of world could we create, what kind of families could we build, if we loved our husbands as we love ourselves? There is, I think, some asymmetry in these rhetorical questions. The thought experiment, "What if my husband loved me as he loves himself?" leads in a different direction than the thought experiment, "What if I loved my husband as I love myself?" This in turn might be interpreted as continuing evidence of the deep cultural chasm between men and women. It could, however, lead us to a quite different conclusion.

Marriage could be viewed as an institution for the mutual growth and education of the partners. According to this vision, the relationship between a husband and wife should lead each of them to greater maturity, depth and perfection. The differences between men and women do not signify the inferiority of one person to the other, but instead illustrate the incompleteness of each person in comparison with the perfection of God. No one gloats over his or her spouse's failings, because each person has failings of their own. Since the job of personal growth is a full-time one, no time is left for focusing on the weaknesses of others. Moreover, we would avoid being judgmental toward our partner, who is in a unique position to help us in our own journey.

The principle of indissoluble marriage is most important in this context. Often, our wish to mask our own faults is quite powerful, as is our capacity for self-deception. When our partners point

---

11 *Ibid.*
12 Mark 12:51; see Milton Steinberg, **Basic Judaism,** 77

us toward areas of potential growth, we often resist listening to their advice. Thus we may run from the relationship at the exact moment when our partner can be of the deepest and most lasting help to us.

COMMENT ON CAROL ROSE

Economists have come to appreciate the fact that the activity that takes place inside the business firm is quite distinct from the activity that takes place among firms in the market place as a whole.[13] Contracts are structured differently inside firms than across firms, pricing mechanisms are used differently, monitoring is done differently, and so forth. It seems to be equally true that the activities that take place between men and women inside the household are quite different, and need to be recognized as distinct from, the activities that take place between men and women in society as a whole.

As Professor Rose notes, there are advantages to both cooperation and retaliation.[14] What Professor Rose does not explicitly note, however, is that each household can benefit from having the ability to play both cooperative and non-cooperative strategies. That is, the household can benefit from having one person who attends to the construction and maintenance of lasting, trusting relationships, both inside the household and outside it. At the same time, the household sometimes needs to make credible threats to the outside world, or to enforce the rules of "tit-for-tat." In short, cooperation is beneficial, but it does not follow that the household, or that any individual ought to cooperate in all circumstances and with all possible players. The household needs both the capacity to cooperate and to retaliate.

It may be that Professor Rose's scenario of the cooperative wife and the rational (i.e. indifferent to others) husband creates the possibility of the household pursuing both strategies. In this event, the husband would play "tit-for-tat" with the outside world, while the wife would maintain the cooperative relationships, both inside the family, and with the (necessarily) small number of trusted people outside it. For this scenario to work, however, there must be trust and a kind of unity of purpose within the marriage. The tendency of the husband to play "tit-for-tat" must somehow be restrained in his relationship with his wife and children. He

---

13 See Ronald Coase, "The Nature of the Firm," **IV Economica** (1937) and the enormous literature spawned by this article

14 Carol Rose, "Bargaining and Gender," **18 Harv. J.L. & Pub.** Pol'y 547 (1995)

must somehow learn to be "other regarding" at least with these significant others. At the same time, the wife's tendency to trust must be restrained so that she does not give away the store, so to speak. Both have something significant to offer the partnership, and each has something significant to learn from the other.

Professor Rose constructs a rather grim scenario in which the non-cooperative partner in the marriage extorts everything from his wife, who is assumed to be the only one concerned with the children.[15]

The more typical "rational" player chooses "tit-for-tat:" he does not cheat unless cheated upon.[16] Thus, Rose's scenario is based upon the marriage unravelling when one person decides to extort all the gains from a relationship that presumably was once mutually beneficial. But an equally grim scenario can be constructed in which the cooperative partner withdraws her co-operation. Game theory shows that if the cooperative partner decides to defect for some reason, the game will unravel almost immediately, as the "tit-for-tat" player will also withdraw his cooperation.[17]

Thus, the conclusion drawn by Professor Rose is not the only one that could be drawn from her framework. She argues that women should acquire more property, specifically so that they will be less inclined to cooperate when it is against their interest to do so.[18] Having income or wealth independently of their husbands allows women to refuse to cooperate with their extortionist husbands. And this is certainly true. But it is equally true that husbands need to learn to cooperate. They need to learn to be willing to pay some price, some of the time, to keep their families together, rather than to extort all the quasi-rents from the partnership.

This bears upon my earlier observations about the relationship between divorce and the labor force. Women with greater income levels can more readily withdraw their cooperation, and when they do, the marriage game unravels unless the man has developed some ability to cooperate. So it seems just as urgent that men learn to cooperate, as that women acquire property. These seem to be parallel tracks that should be pursued.

I think that one of the problems with the traditional marriage was that the partners became overly specialized emotionally as well as economically. Perhaps it will seem strange for an economist

---

15   *Ibid.*, at 561-63
16   Douglas G. Baird, **Game Theory and the Law** (1994)
17   *Ibid.*
18   Rose, *supra note* 14, at 561

to criticize specialization and division of labor. But it is my considered opinion that we can easily overdo it. We might describe
the emotional division of labor in tradtitional marriages in the
following way: the mother is in charge of all the relationships inside the family, sometimes monitoring and controlling even the
sibling relationships, while the father is in charge of the family's
relationships with the outside world. The benefit of this specialization is that each of them does what they are most comfortable
doing. The cost of it is that they missed many opportunities to
learn from each other's strengths. They spend a lot of time trying
to get the other to behave as they would, rather than appreciat-
ing the unique contributions the other makes to the partnership.
And indeed, trying to "get the other person to change," is quite a
different activity from being willing to change yourself.

CONCLUSION - MISSED OPPORTUNITIES

If we had chosen "Live a Balanced Life" as our slogan, the whole
feminist movement could have had a distinctly Aristotelian ring
to it.[19] If we had chosen "Love Your Neighbor as Yourself" as our
approach, the feminist movement could have drawn upon the best
of Christianity. In either of these approaches, we would have been
drawing upon the best, deepest, and most thoughtful aspects of
our traditions. Instead, we chose "Having it All" as our slogan
and equality of income as our goal. In so doing, we embraced a
shallow materialism and a mindless egalitarianism.

In short, I believe that the women's movement has missed some
opportunities. We could have humanized the workplace; instead
we bureaucraticized the home. We demand that our husbands
be like ourselves, sometimes creating elaborate implicit or even
explicit accounting systems to ensure that they do so?[20] We demand child care, so that we can leave the home and compete with
men at work. We abandon the best that is in us, so that we can
emulate the worst that is in men. When we harden our hearts to
place a six week old baby into the care of strangers, who will moderate us? The opportunity for a different kind of women's movement still exists, however. The alternative visions that I suggest
are still within our reach. These visions lie within our power to
choose. We can address the universal issues of work and mar-

---

19 See *supra* text accompanying notes 10-11
20 See, e.g., Gillian K. Hadfield, "Households at Work: Beyond Labor Market
    Policies to Remedy the Gender Gap," 82 **Georgetown Law Journal** (1993)
    (arguing that economists and lawyers should study the household division of
    labor more thoroughly, with an eye toward reform, because labor market
    interventions will never by themselves adequately remedy the gender gap).

riage in different ways. Instead of increasing women's financial security as a means of coping with the instability of marriage, we could work on improving our marriages. Our mothers could have benefitted from better marriages, and so could we.

But this different kind of women's movement requires a very different mindset. We need to face some of the basic realities of the human condition: our finiteness and our imperfection. We need to let go of the illusion that we can and should change everything and everyone around us. This distracts us from our primary task of changing ourselves in all the many ways that we can be changed for the better. We need to trust that if we change our corner of the world, we really are doing our part to create a better world.

Ultimately, these are the truly rational choices for us.

Originally published:
Harvard Journal of Law & Public Policy
Spring 1995

At the time of this writing, Dr. Morse was the John M. Olin Visiting Scholar at Cornell Law School, and an Associate Professor of Economics at George Mason University.

~ 18 ~

Living With the Sandwich We Made

THE SANDWICH GENERATION IS one of the more frivolous complaints of the baby-boom generation — as if we were the first generation in history to have both children and parents!

The sandwich isn't the problem. The problem is having two dependent generations at the same time. That is unique in the history of the human race. But why is it unique to us?

I'll tell you why. It is one of the unintended consequences of the revolution in contraceptive technology.

This technology, including the pill and legalized abortion, made delaying childbearing easier for larger numbers of people. Popping a pill is a lot simpler than self-restraint. It is hardly surprising that the age of first marriage and the age of first childbearing have both steadily risen since the 1960s. This creates a chronological spread across generations. That spread is responsible for the so-called sandwich generation.

Let me illustrate by telling my story. Like many women of my generation, I postponed childbearing until my career was established. I thought it was smart and responsible to be independent. I was 38 when I had my first child.

Let's do a bit of simple math. My mom was 31 when she had me. (I was the third of six kids, by the way. She wasn't just getting started.) By the time I had my first, my mom was in her 60s. If I had had my first child 10 years sooner, I'd have been 28, not an early age at first childbirth.

But look at the difference those 10 years would have made to my mom. Instead of being in her 60s, she'd be in her 50s. Instead of being infirm when I have school-aged kids, she'd be young enough to enjoy them and, incidentally, to help out.

Likewise, by the time she got old enough to need significant help from me and my siblings, my kids would be teenagers. I wouldn't be driving them to ball games and dance classes; they could drive themselves places. In fact, they might even be some help with their grandparents.

Multiply my personal decisions by hundreds of women. The age at first childbirth has risen steadily in the last 20 years, even though out-of-wedlock births and teen pregnancy have continued to be a problem. Both economic pressures and the cultural ethos encourage women to delay childbearing and to have only one or two children.

This might be workable for a subset of families. Indeed, there has always been tremendous variation in this kind of very private decision making.

But the society-wide trend is creating a situation that is not sustainable for an entire society. As the process continues, women like me won't have a batch of siblings to help take care of grandma. There will be one or two adult children, taking care of at least two sets of elderly parents, or even more if the grandparents have divorced and remarried. These same adults will also be taking care of young children.

The only possible result of this trend will be some form of institutional care for either the very old or the very young, or both. There simply will not be enough hands on deck inside the family to take care of that many dependent people simultaneously. A family with shorter spacing between the generations would be able to stagger the care of its dependent members across time.

The very youngest generation wouldn't be dependent infants at the same time the oldest generation is most in need of care.

My daughter recently asked me, "Mom, how old should I be when I get married and have kids?"

I said to her, "Well, Honey, I was 38 when you were born. If you are 38 when you have your first child, how old will I be?"

I gave her a minute to do the math. "Seventy-six."

"Right. If you wait that long, you may have me and your baby in diapers at the same time. But, do whatever you want."

I sympathize, up to a point, with the pressures of the sandwich generation. Really, I do. I have a couple of school-age kids as well as aging parents and in-laws. My mother-in-law lived with us for the last six months of her life. She had cancer and Alzheimer's.

But I don't think it appropriate for me to complain about doing "double-duty" in the sandwich generation. I was not very realistic. Most of my generation didn't think too closely about the fact that our parents would get old and become legitimately dependent on us.

When Thomas Malthus suggested marrying later in life as a means of controlling population growth, he was in effect suggesting a whole lot of delayed sexual gratification. Not surprisingly, few people took his suggestion seriously enough to actually implement it in their own lives.

But today, delayed childbearing doesn't necessarily represent responsible delayed gratification. Quite often, that late age of first childbearing represents the results of 10, 15 or maybe even 20 years of contracepted sex. We had our fun. Now it's time to pay. We discipline our kids by giving them the "natural consequences" of their actions. We are in this sandwich generation because we didn't do the math. Now we are getting the natural consequences of the choices we made long ago.

© National Catholic Register

---

*Originally published: National Catholic Register
March, 2004*

---

http://www.ncregister.com/site/article/living_with_the_sandwich_we_made/#ixzz3OovGm7DQ –

Reprinted with permission

SECTION D
THE PROBLEMS OF THE CAREER WOMAN

~ 19 ~

Home Alone America

WHAT IS IT ABOUT the chattering classes anyhow? Why can the policy wonks and public intellectuals not see the point of Mary Eberstadt's important new book, *Home Alone America?* Many reviewers seem determined to miss the deep truth of this book: It would be better for both children and adults if more American parents were with their kids more of the time.

Raising a child is first and foremost about building a relationship with the child. The most important aspect of parenting is relational. The family is all about relationships, not about the transfer of resources. Children need a relationship with their parents far more than they need any specific resources from them. The social significance of parenting goes far beyond Big People Transferring Resources to Little People.

To make this point, Mary Eberstadt looks at Sex and Drugs and Rock and Roll. Literally. In her chapter about the sexual behavior of teenagers, she makes the case that teen sexual activity is correlated with being Home Alone, unsupervised by adults. (Well, duh!) She dissects the cheerleading over the declines in teen pregnancy and abortion. She shows that these declines, welcome though they are, do not indicate that all is well on the teenager sex scene.

For instance, many kids are having oral sex instead of vaginal intercourse. Now, it is certainly true that no one has ever gotten pregnant from oral sex. However, many people do get sexually transmitted diseases (STDs) from oral sex. Condoms are not much help in preventing the spread of viruses that are transmitted orally.

Rock and roll lyrics reveal the lost souls of teens abandoned by their parents. Making disapproval noises about the vile lyrics of rap music is almost a sport in some adult circles. But Eberstadt cautions us against simply dismissing what she calls "the primal scream of teenage music." Notorious rappers such as Eminem, Snoop Dog and Jay-Z, save their most obnoxious lyrics for the fathers who abandoned them and the mothers who neglected them. Coincidence? Mary Eberstadt thinks not.

The chapter on drugs is not about illegal drug use, in which

99

kids medicate themselves. Eberstadt instead looks at the use of legal drugs, in which adults medicate children to make them more manageable. Whether it is ritalin to control Attention Deficit Disorder, or anti-depressants to make kids feel better, Eberstadt feels sure that the increase in prescription of these drugs can be connected with the fact that more and more kids are left to fend for themselves for more and more hours each day.

The "Zoloft killer" could be a poster child for *Home Alone America*. You remember Christopher Pittman, of course. At the age of twelve, he shot his sleeping grandparents, and set fire to their house. During his recent trial, his attorneys tried to argue that he was under the influence of Zoloft, and was therefore not responsible for the killings and the arson.

But while the media chose to focus on the medication angle, the real story was left unmentioned. Why is a 12-year-old on anti-depressant medication in the first place? And why was he living with his grandparents? He was abandoned by his mother in infancy. He was passed from one family member to another. His father was described as a "stern disciplinarian." The boy had run away from home, threatened suicide and was placed in a psychiatric center in Florida for six days before moving in with his grandparents. He ultimately shot his grandparents because he was angry that they disciplined him for trying to choke another child on the school bus. This was a troubled child, medication or no medication. Is it a coincidence that he was abandoned by his mother?

I don't mean to give the impression that *Home Alone America* is a doom and gloom book. It is, above all, a generous book. The point of these dire stories is not that every child in day care will end up as a serial killer. Rather, the point is that this is the wrong question. We owe it to ourselves and to our children to set the standards of care higher than simply avoiding dire outcomes.

So forget the clueless chattering classes and go buy this book. If your family has one or more parent committed to spending the majority of their time in the home for the benefit of the kids, you need this book. It will affirm the importance of what you are doing. If you are sometimes lonely because you are the only stay at home mom in the neighborhood, so your kids have no one to play with after school, *Home Alone America* will tell you you are doing the right thing. If you are on the edge of wondering whether it really is worth the effort to keep your high-powered job going, whether the extra income (after taxes and working expenses) is really worth the stress involved in a two-earner household, this book will encourage you.

If your adult children are struggling with these questions, buy this book for them. If your heart has been breaking while you watch your grandchildren flounder while your adult children try to figure out all this stuff for themselves, give them this book. If you know someone who is expecting a baby and wondering what to do, give them this book. If you are a teacher, or counselor or therapist, and you are wondering why you are seeing so many disturbed, angry and unhappy children, get this book. If anyone ever asks your advice about any of these questions, and you aren't sure what to say, read this book, and give it away.

Home Alone America could be the book that tips the scales finally in favor of more generosity toward children and family. Don't miss out on being part of that trend.

© National Catholic Register

Originally published: iFeminists.com
May of 2005

Available at: http://www.ifeminists.net/introduction/editorials/2005/0525morse.html - Reprinted with permission

SECTION E
SEX EDUCATION

~ 20 ~

Does Anything Work in Sex Education?

A study shows that abstinence education programs don't work. They had the same failure rate as contraceptive programs. Doesn't that show neither of them works?

ABSTINENCE EDUCATION DOESN'T WORK. That was the big hoopla in the American press over the publication of a study by *Mathematica*, purporting to show that abstinence education programs don't work. But with a bit of checking, I found something you are not likely to hear on the evening news. Sex education programs don't "work" either.[1]

Let me give a bit of background for the benefit of readers not immersed in U.S. politics over the funding of sex programs. The federal government began funding abstinence education programs in 1998. This, after many years and millions of dollars spent funding programs that teach contraception as a neutral technology that fourth graders can choose to use or not as their wisdom decrees. In the last election, the Democrats took control of Congress. Given their record on moral issues, it is likely they will reduce or eliminate the funding for abstinence education. Their move will be to fund only "comprehensive sex education," which in practice means programs that teach contraception first, sexual activity as an entitlement and abstinence as an afterthought.

If those are the alternatives, it is fair to ask whether sex-ed programs are any more successful than abstinence programs. Let's listen to some experts.

A 2002 study published in the *British Medical Journal* examined 26 programs that included school based programs, multi-faceted programs, family planning and clinic based programs, as well as abstinence programs in the U.S. and Canada. The results: "The interventions did not delay initiation of sexual intercourse in young women or young men, did not improve the use of birth control at every intercourse, or at last intercourse for either men or women, did not reduce pregnancy rates in young women."[2]

---

1   "Impact of Four Title V, Section 510 Abstinence Education Programs," **Mathematica**, April 2007. Available on-line at: http://aspe.hhs.gov/hsp/abstinence07/index.cfm

2   Di Censo, Alba, et al. "Interventions to reduce unintended pregnancies among adolescents: systematic review of randomized controlled

Another study of a very well-designed and well-delivered sex-ed program in Scotland was also published in the BMJ. The result: "When the intervention group was compared with the conventional sex education group, there were no differences in sexual activity or sexual risk taking by the age of 16 years."[3]

Then there is Douglas Kirby's 2001 survey of over 300 programs of all sorts. "Most studies of school-based and school-linked health centers revealed no effect on student sexual behavior or contraceptive use."[4]

Finding programs that don't work is not very difficult. Programs based in schools, whether of the sex-ed or abstinence variety, do not work very well at reducing teen pregnancy. Adults coming into the classroom and yammering about sex, whether for it or agin' it, just do not have much impact on teens.

When you think about it, this is not surprising. We know from other kinds of studies that the biggest protective factors for delaying teen sex are married parents and religious observance. Some of the sex-ed studies confirm this by showing that within their little samples, family composition and parental supervision, parental expectations for behavior are among the biggest protective factors. In other words, what is going on at home completely dwarfs anything that is going on at school. As Dr. Trevor Stammers, a wise British commentator put it: "Much teenage sex has little do with sex itself, but is connected with searching for meaning, identity and belonging."[5]

That is why some of the more successful programs include substantial after school and community-based components. The Best Friends abstinence program, for instance, is not a classroom-based curriculum. It promotes abstinence among teens from inner-city school districts by fostering self-respect and sound decision-making. It includes mentoring for at least 45 minutes a

trials," **British Medical Journal** 324, 15 June 2002

3   Wight, Daniel, et al. "Limits of teacher delivered sex education: interim behavioral outcomes from randomized trial." **British Medical Journal** 324, 15 June 2002
4   Kirby, Douglas, "Understanding What Works and What Doesn't in Reducing Adolescent Sexual Risk-Taking," **Family Planning Perspectives** 33(6): 276-81, (November/ December 2001). Available on-line at: http://www.guttmacher.org/pubs/journals/3327601.html
5   Stammers, Trevor, "Sexual health in adolescents," **British Medical Journal** 334, 20 January 2007

week, group discussions every three weeks, role model presentation, and enrollment in fitness and dance classes. It has had great
success at reducing teen pregnancy both at the middle school
and high school levels.[6]

Some successful programs don't even talk about sex. Douglas
Kirby again: "One group of effective programs were service learning programs. These programs include voluntary or unpaid service in the community (eg, tutoring, working as a teachers' aide
or working in nursing homes) and structured time for prepara-
tion and reflection before, during and after service, (e.g. group
discussions, journal writing or papers). ...(S)tudies, have consistently indicated that service learning either delays sexual activity
or reduces teenage pregnancy. However, not all service learning
programs addressed sexual or contraceptive behavior. Why then
did they change behavior? ...

"There are many plausible explanations. The programs may in
fact have increased connectedness to caring adults (some of whom
may have expressed clear norms about avoiding sex)...they may
have increased autonomy, or they may simply have occupied a
fair amount of discretionary time during which the students might
have otherwise been unsupervised at home and might have engaged in unprotected sex."

If it is possible to reduce teen pregnancy without even discuss-
ing sex, I am not particularly troubled about a report on just four
abstinence programs which have already been superseded by
other, more sophisticated programs. Even the *Mathematica* study
does not denigrate abstinence programs, but instead emphasiz-
es: "Some policymakers and health educators have questioned
whether the Title V, Section 510 programs' focus on abstinence
elevates STD risks. Findings from this study suggest that this is
not the case, as program youth are no more likely to engage in
unprotected sex than their control group counterparts."

The real questions about abstinence education are these. Given
that family structure and religious practice are significant protective factors against teen sexual activity, shouldn't the federal government support marriage and religion? Given that many, many
sex-ed programs do nothing to reduce teen pregnancy, why are
we even considering pouring more federal money into Planned
Parenthood-type organizations to promote their ideology of hu-

---

6   Young, Michael and Penhollow, Tina, "The Impact of Abstinence Education:
What does the Research Say?" **American Journal of Health Education** 37(4)
July/August 2006, 194-202.

man sexuality? And if we are going to pump money into sex-ed programs of dubious value and even more dubious values—why isn't it a slam dunk that we should fund abstinence programs at an equal level?

Of course, there is one other possibility. Given that human connectedness is what kids seek in sex, the federal government could stop spending any money at all on sending ladies into classrooms to hector the kids about sex. We could leave this very human problem to the states, localities, or school boards.

Or we could even leave it to parents to talk to their kids about sex.

Just a thought.

Originally published: MercatorNet.com
May 1, 2007

---

available on-line at: http://www.mercatornet.com/articles/view/does_anything_work_in_sex_
education#sthash.H3RorvTL.dpuf - Reprinted with permission

~ 21 ~

Get the Government
Out of Sex Ed

IF YOU NEED AN operation and the doctor tells you that overall, seven-eighths of patients have a successful outcome, you might think that was a pretty good deal. But suppose the operation failed. While you're in the recovery room, the doctor tells you, "Oh, by the way, for people like you, the operation only succeeds 30% of the time. But we'll sell you the solution to the botched operation." You'd be furious. You'd sue that doctor for malpractice if you didn't punch him first.

Yet this is precisely the situation Congress supports by funding Planned Parenthood and its allies to provide "comprehensive sex education" in secondary schools.

This is no exaggeration. Look at contraceptive failure rates, using Planned Parenthood's own data. Two studies, (listed below, with website addresses) use this definition of contraceptive failure: the percentage of women who experience a pregnancy at the end of one year of using a particular contraceptive method. Somewhere between 12% and 13% of all contracepting women experienced a pregnancy within a year. In other words, about seven-eighths of women use contraceptives successfully. Two of the most commonly used and widely promoted methods are oral contraceptives and the male condom. Of all women using the Pill for one year, somewhere around 8% will experience a pregnancy. Between 14% and 15% of women who use the condom will become pregnant within a year.

But these statistics, while technically correct, don't tell the whole story, not by a long shot. These are the "overall" statistics that our hypothetical doctor used in our opening story. The "for people like you" statistics paint a very different picture. These studies break down the population into age groups, income levels, marital status and race.

A poor cohabiting teenager using the Pill has a failure rate of 48.4%. You read that correctly: nearly half of poor cohabiting teenagers get pregnant during their first year using the Pill. If she kicked her boyfriend out of the house, or if she married him, her probability of pregnancy drops to 12.9%. At the other extreme, a middle-aged, middle-class married woman has a 3% chance of getting pregnant after a year on the Pill.

Over 70% of poor, cohabiting teenagers using condoms, will be pregnant within a year. By contrast, the middle-aged, middle-class married woman has a 6% chance of pregnancy after a year of condom use.

These figures cast new light on the debate over contraception education. The commonly quoted failure rates of 8% for the Pill and 15% for the condom are inflated by the highly successful use by middle-aged, middle-class married couples. Yet, the government promotes contraception most heavily among the young, the poor and the single. The "overall failure rates" are simply not relevant to this target population.

Planned Parenthood and its allies in the sex education business have had conniptions over federal funding for abstinence education. But at least abstinence actually works. If you don't have sex, you won't get pregnant. It works every time.

With contraception, we can absolutely predict that some sexual encounters will result in pregnancy. The young, the poor and the unmarried are the most likely to experience a contraceptive failure. For these groups, pregnancy is not a rare accident, but highly likely. When the inevitable pregnancy occurs, guess who is ready to help solve her problem? That's right: Planned Parenthood will sell her an abortion. The same people who teach sex education, which increases the demand for purchasing contraception, also sell the "solution" to contraceptive failure, which is abortion. Yet the federal government spends about $12 on contraceptive-related programs to every $1 spent on abstinence education.

We don't give federal grants to tobacco companies to teach students "low-risk" forms of smoking on the grounds that "kids are going to smoke anyway." We shouldn't be giving federal grants to groups that sell contraception, to teach kids to use contraception.

It is time for the federal government to get out of the sex education business once and for all.

"Contraceptive Failure in the First Two Years of Use: Differences Across Socioeconomic Subgroups," Nalini Ranjit, Akinrinola Bankole, Jacqueline E. Darroch and Susheela Singh. **Family Planning Perspectives,** Vol 33, No. 1. January/February 2001, pp. 19-27.
"Contraceptive Failure Rates: New Estimates From the 1995 National Survey of Family Growth," Haisahn Fu, Jacqueline E. Darroch, Taylor Haas, and

Nalini Ranjit, **Family Planning Perspectives,** Vol 31, No. 2. March/April 1999, pp. 56-63.

Originally published: Townhall
July 9, 2007

Available on-line at: http://townhall.com/columnists/jenniferrobackmorse/2007/07/09/get_the_government_out_of_sex_ed/page/full - Reprinted with permission

Like a stake in the ground...

Natural marriage limits the state.

~ 22 ~

Comprehensive Abstinence Education

THE RUNNING DISPUTE BETWEEN abstinence education and comprehensive sex education flares up at least once a year around budget request time.

Comprehensive sex education programs claim to teach abstinence as the primary strategy, but also teach contraceptive use, just in case. "Abstinence only doesn't work," we are continually told.

I recently spoke at a conference of remarkable young people that made me think that conventional classroom-based abstinence education does need something else. Call it: comprehensive abstinence education.

The conference was sponsored by Singles for Christ, an organization of college students and other young adults. About a hundred young people gathered at a university in southern California to talk about being "100% Pure," and about how "True Love Waits." Singles for Christ is an offshoot of Couples for Christ, an international organization founded in the Philippines.

While sitting at my book table, I was approached by a non-conference-going student from another University of California system school. She identified herself as a "student sex educator." She wanted to pick up the literature, to see what information we were promoting.

I imagine she was expecting to find the stereotypes of abstinence education: Scare kids away from sex. Keep them ignorant about self-protection. Wring your hands when the kids get pregnant or infected.

That is when it struck me what was so remarkable about this abstinence conference. It didn't talk about avoiding pregnancy or STDs. Instead, the Singles for Christ conference talked about marriage: how to prepare for marriage, and how to choose a partner wisely.

On second thought, maybe it isn't comprehensive abstinence education, after all. Comprehensive marriage education offers the most complete and appealing message of hope to the next generation.

113

The very first presentation of the conference was by a young married couple with three small children. They talked about meeting at a Singles for Christ event and about their courtship. They didn't have to say they loved each other and their children. Anyone could see that for themselves.

But it was more than the presentations that convinced me there was something special going on here. It was also watching the young people interacting among themselves. They were singing, laughing and teasing each other. No downcast up-tight virgins here. These kids were obviously having a blast.

I thought to myself: I bet this program "succeeds" in all the measures that Congress expects of federally funded sex-ed programs: a lower rate of non-marital births, a later age at sexual debut and fewer STDs.

The genius of the Singles for Christ program is that the young people are brought up within a social network of shared expectations. Most of the Singles for Christ were probably Kids for Christ or Youth for Christ. They probably have married parents who are Couples for Christ or widowed grandmothers who are Handmaidens for Christ. When they were teenagers, probably very few went home to empty houses, turned on a TV porn channel, and had unsupervised afternoons after school.

This abstinence program is more than a classroom experience. This is a full way of life that provides young people with an appealing future as part of a married couple.

The lessons are embedded in a community of supportive adults, who expect certain behavior and model that behavior. The adults prepare the young to participate in the adult life of the community, on the community's terms.

I have seen this model before.

I saw it in the group of Chinese Baptist students I encountered at Berkeley, of all places. Their pastor and his wife discouraged dating, and encouraged socializing in groups. I saw it last month in a Catholic student group at Florida State University. Run by a religious order called the Brothers of Hope, these young people are getting married in their early 20s and starting families. They are too busy to be messing around getting into sexual trouble. Their sex lives are directed toward enhancing their marriages and creating families.

This is why the political battles over government-funded sex education are so fierce. Each side is promoting a whole way of life. Modern sex education prepares the young for a lifetime of casual sexual encounters that have no future.

The norm in our society is that sex is a sterile activity, with babies thrown in as an afterthought if you happen to like that sort of thing. If you do get pregnant, it isn't a big deal, since you can kill the baby if you feel you need to.

The socially responsible way of having a baby is to carefully plan it for your 30s after you've established the real business of your life, namely business.

Having sex with someone who would be a disaster as a mate or co-parent is now considered normal. The sexual social contract is approximately, "I will allow you to use me, if you allow me to use you."

Broken hearts are collateral damage to the sexual revolution. The best message on offer is "Protect yourself from STDs. Try not to get pregnant. Other than that, you are on your own."

The advocates of abstinence education have a better, more hopeful message, that goes beyond merely abstaining from sex. The message is that marriage is attainable: "You can get married and stay married. Your children can spend their entire childhoods with both their parents, married to each other. This way of life is possible and desirable."

On second thought, maybe it isn't comprehensive abstinence education, after all. Comprehensive marriage education offers the most complete and appealing message of hope to the next generation.

© National Catholic Register

*Originally published: National Catholic Register
January, 2008*

116

SECTION F
COHABITATION

~ 23 ~

The Incredible Shrinking Household

I WAS SADDENED BY RECENT news stories confirming that the number of cohabitating couples continues to rise.

Many young people who have survived their parents' divorces are longing for life-long love, but have no idea how to make it work. Many of these young people see cohabitation as a way of avoiding a costly mistake that could lead to divorce.

Research shows that couples who cohabit before marriage are more likely to report unhappiness in their marriages, and more likely to divorce. This result surprises some people, including the researchers that have uncovered it. But it is not a surprise when you consider that the marriage relationship is much more than a glorified roommate or business relationship. People imagine they are taking their potential spouse for a "test drive." The problem is that you cannot simulate commitment. Live-in lovers tend to have one foot out the door throughout the relationship.

Then, too, cohabiters only pretend to practice self-giving; in reality, they hold back from one another. Untrusting, uncommitted, they rehearse for a show that may never go on.

I am sorry to say that I know this from experience. My husband and I lived together before we married. It has taken us a long time to overcome some of the habits we developed during those early years. I would have been just as surprised as the researchers who found the cohabitation is a poor predictor of successful marriage. But since I have experienced cohabitation, marriage with reservations, as well as self-giving marriage with abandon, I think I have a pretty good handle on what the research data actually mean.

While this is essentially a cultural and spiritual problem, there is an economic aspect to the issue. The rising prosperity of the Western world, coupled with the increasing economic opportunities for women in particular, makes living alone more financially feasible than it used to be. This rising prosperity is one of the factors at work in a number of the census trends. People are living alone: Nearly a third of all households consist of individuals or unrelated individuals.

I would never say that this prosperity is a bad thing. Many of the

119

Founding Fathers, for instance, were unsure whether a "commercial republic" could be stable, since wealthy people would tend to become complacent. I do think that we need to pay closer attention to the choices we are making surrounding our families, or we will all end up alone.

The correlation of child well-being and living with both biological parents is present in the raw data of most studies. The debate among scholars centers on the extent to which this can be accounted for by differences in resources typically found in single-parent households. The debate then turns to ways in which society can offer additional resources to support the children of single mothers. But most studies show that children of single parents still do worse even after accounting for differences in economic status. This suggests that the children are harmed from the loss of the relationship itself, not simply the loss of resources.

It is almost as if policy makers and academics wish they could find any way possible to help children, short of stating the obvious fact that they would be better off if their parents were married. The goal seems to be to find the minimal set of human relationships that a child can have and still turn out tolerably well, or to find the least adults must do for their children. This minimalist posture is not confined to academic advocates and people who themselves are divorced. People from across the political spectrum seem to be saying, "What do I have to do in order to maintain my position that divorce or single parenthood is not harmful to children? How much money does society have to spend to make up for the loss of the relationship, so that I will not have to give up my belief that parents are entitled to any lifestyle choices they want?"

The crucial cultural issue behind the "home-alone" family is the American ethos of independence. We tend to glorify and glamorize independence. Independence is all well and good, but the truth is that there are times when we are legitimately dependent on others. The human person comes into the world as a helpless infant. Most modern political theory treats this as if it were a peripheral fact. Children require a social order around them for their very survival. The family provides that life-giving structure that allows the infant to thrive and ultimately to develop into the kind of person who can safely be turned loose in a free society.

Americans tend to be uncomfortable with the vulnerability that comes from acknowledging our dependence on others. We prefer the illusion of control. In my view, we would benefit from developing our ability to be interdependent with others in a constructive way. I believe that, for many people, fear of being dependent stands in the way of healthy cooperation. This is what destroys our self-giving nature, and, ultimately, undermines the welfare and happiness of our families.

© National Catholic Register

Originally published: National Catholic Register
August 26, 2001

~ 24 ~

Why Not Take Her For a test Drive?

RESEARCH SHOWS THAT COHABITATION is correlated with unhappiness and domestic violence. Cohabiting couples report lower levels of satisfaction in the relationship than married couples. Women are more likely to be abused by a cohabiting boyfriend than a husband. Children are more likely to abused by their mothers' boyfriends than by her husband, even if the boyfriend is their biological father. If a cohabiting couple ultimately marries, they have a higher propensity to divorce.

Most of the recent reports and commentaries on cohabitation report these difficulties, and at the same time, tend to downplay them. Living together before marriage seems to resemble taking a car for a test drive. The "trial period" gives people a chance to discover whether they are compatible. "You wouldn't buy a car without taking it for a test drive, now would you?"

Here's the problem with the car analogy: the car doesn't have hurt feelings if the driver dumps it back at the used car lot and decides not to buy it. The analogy works great if you picture yourself as the driver. It stinks if you picture yourself as the car.

Yet this is the implication of the "test drive" metaphor. I am going to drive you around the block a few times, withholding judgement and commitment until I have satisfied myself about you. Pay no attention to my indecision, or my periodic evaluations of your performance. Try to act as if we were married, so I can get a clear picture of what you're likely to be like as a spouse. You just pretend to be married; I'll just pretend to be shopping.

The contract analogy doesn't help much either. Living together is fine as long as both people agree to it. The agreement amounts to this: "I am willing to let you use me as if I were a commodity, as long as you allow me to treat you as if you were a commodity." But this is a bogus agreement. We can say at the outset that we agree to be the "man of steel", but no one can credibly promise to have no feelings of remorse if the relationship fails.

There is an essential difference between sexual activity and other forms of activity. The sexual act is by its nature, a gift of oneself to another person. We all have a deep longing to be cherished by the person we have sex with. That longing is not fooled by our

SECTION F
COHABITATION

pretensions to sophistication.

Here is a better analogy: Suppose I ask you to give me a blank check, signed and ready to cash. All I have to do is fill in the amount. Most people would be unlikely to do this. You might do it, if you snuck out and drained the money out of your account before you gave me the check. Or, you could give me the check and be scared about what I might do.

But what do you have in your checking account that is more valuable than what you give to a sexual partner? When people live together, and sleep together, without marriage, they put themselves in a position that is similar to the person being asked to give a blank check. They either hold back on their partner by not giving the full self in the sexual act and in their shared lives together. Or, they feel scared a lot of the time, wondering whether their partner will somehow take advantage of their vulnerability.

No one can simulate self-giving. Half a commitment is no commitment. Cohabiting couples have one foot out the door, throughout the relationship. They rehearse not trusting. The social scientists that gather the data do not have an easy way to measure this kind of dynamic inside the relationship.

In my view, this accounts for the disappointing results of cohabitation. I am sorry to say that I learned this from experience. My husband and I lived together before we were married. It took us a long time to unlearn the habits of the heart that we built up during those cohabiting years.

The sexual revolution promised a humane and realistic approach to human sexuality. Ironically, the uncommitted-sex mentality has proven to underestimate both the value and the power of sexual activity. Lifelong, committed relationships are difficult, no doubt about it. But self-giving loving relationships still have the best chance of making us happy.

*Originally published: Boundless in 2001,
republished at their new website
on December 19, 2012*

Available on-line at: http://www.boundless.org/relationships/2012/why-not-take-her-for-a-test-drive - Reprinted with permission

~ 25 ~

Cohabitation Is a Social Injustice

A S EVERYONE KNOWS, MARRIAGE is an outdated, fossilized, oppressive institution that is constantly changing under our feet, evolving into a freer and higher and better form. And if it isn't morphing into one of its alternatives, we would be better off without it.

As everyone doesn't know, social science can now show that the "alternatives to marriage" don't work. A recent news story brought this home in a particularly vivid fashion for that most fashionable of alternatives to marriage: cohabitation.

In Dallas, a mother and her boyfriend were arrested after three of her children were found in a hotel room, starved and abused. The facts of the case fit in with the general pattern of knowledge about the hazards of cohabitation. This story puts a human face on the statistics.

First, we know that a cohabiting boyfriend is the person most likely to abuse a child. From British child-abuse registries, we learn that a child living with his or her mother and a live-in boyfriend is 33 times more likely to be abused than a child living with his or her biological married parents. From a study of inflicted injury deaths in Missouri, we learn that children living in households with unrelated adults were 50 times more likely to die of inflicted injuries than households with both biological parents present.

In 82% of the cases, the "unrelated adult" was the mother's cohabiting boyfriend.

So it was in this case. The boyfriend was the perpetrator. While the mother was out working, he sexually abused her daughter. And although the mother was certainly complicit in locking the kids in the bathroom, the boyfriend was the one beating them.

Speaking of her working, this boyfriend stayed "home" in the hotel room, while the woman went out to work each day. This, too, fits the statistical pattern. Cohabiting men have half the income of married men and work fewer hours.

Each one of the four children had different fathers. The boyfriend's child, needless to say, was not locked in the bathroom with the other kids. This case illustrates the new phenomenon that demographers have identified. They call it "multiple-partner fertility." One of the problems associated with multiple-partner fertility is the relationship of each new boyfriend to the children of the previous boyfriends. To not put too fine a point on it: He is interested in the woman, not in her children from past relationships. The children are leftovers from a previous relationship.

You may object that some of these problems are associated with poverty. And that is partly true. But the deeper truth is that channeling sexual behavior and childbearing into marriage creates wealth rather than dissipates it. Men behave differently when they marry, especially when they become married fathers.

When I give campus talks on the risks of cohabitation, I can always count on some smarty to challenge me saying that the risks are not really so great to people like himself. What he usually means (and it is almost always a "he") is that the statistics are skewed by a large number of poor, uneducated cohabiting couples who are at higher risk for all sorts of problems anyway. Unspoken, but implied, is that he is cohabiting himself and plans not to change based on anything I say.

So, he might argue, this particular boyfriend was just a loser, while the cohabiting men of his own social circle are not. Women of higher income and education will not face such serious problems as this woman living in a hotel room with a creep. But studies that control for education and income still find that cohabitation is risky.

We have created a culture that says sex, marriage and childbearing have no necessary relationship to each other. This culture, like any culture, is made up of the decisions of all of us: the things we choose to do and not do, the justifications we offer for our actions, the things we celebrate and the things we condemn. We have an indirect impact on the culture and therefore on the people around us. Every problem of the poor is exacerbated by the failure of marriage. The "alternatives to marriage" are destroying the culture of the poor.

So I present this challenge to my young friends on campus: "You might get away with participating in social practices that become much more destructive as they trickle down into the lower classes. It is not social justice to claim for yourself the rights to behaviors that you can manage but are a disaster for the less fortunate. Do you want to be part of the solution or part of the problem?"

© National Catholic Register

Originally published: National Catholic Register
November 2009

http://www.ncregister.com/site/article/how_cohabitation_is_a_sin_against_social_
justice/#ixzz3OpSZSAsF - Reprinted with permission

Cohabiting with regrets?
"He doesn't want to get married."
"He doesn't want children."
"Are my peak childbearing years behind me?"

Join us as we Inspire
the Survivors of
the Sexual Revolution!
www.RuthNewsletter.org

SECTION G
DIVORCE

~ 26 ~

Family First

D R. PHIL'S NEW BOOK *Family First* has one feature that sets it apart from the crowded shelves of family self-help books: his chapter on divorced and blended families. He has seen first hand that the official line we've been given about divorce and remarriage is misleading at best and down-right false at worst. You know the "happy talk" I'm talking about: Divorce is no problem, if....

If the mother has enough money, if she spends enough time with the kids, they'll do just fine. If the parents continue to work together in a loving cooperative way, the children will be better off than with a family life of continual strife. If the stepdad is loving and attentive, remarriage is no problem for kids. If the children know that their parents love them, they will have minimal difficulties adjusting to the necessary changes in their parents' lives.

Dr. Phil knows from experience that those huge "ifs" don't automatically occur in real life. Making those "ifs" come true takes an almost super-human effort. Because he is a positive type of guy, he doesn't focus on the negatives. But by spelling out in detail what the biological and stepparents need to do and not do, he makes it clear that divorce, remarriage and stepparenting is no picnic.

Many apologists for easy divorce used to assume that a lack of money caused the problems of single parenting. But social scientists who study family patterns closely are no longer so sanguine. They have found, for instance, that adding a stepparent to a single parent home does increase the financial resources available to the child, but that the presence of stepparents doesn't necessarily help the child. In fact, in some ways the stepparent situation is more complicated and difficult than the single parent situation. Specifically, children with stepparents are more likely to have emotional problems. Dr. Phil's material gives a clue as to why that might be the case.

He states, for instance, "It is my strong belief that unless you as the stepparent are added to the family when the children are very young, it will most likely be very difficult for you to discipline your spouse's children." Now, what kinds of observation might have led Dr. Phil to that conclusion?

He has seen, and I bet you have too, situations in which the kids resent discipline from the stepparent. A child disturbed by his parents' divorce can make family life hell on earth. A wounded child can disrupt his or her parent's new marriage. It is easy enough to understand the dynamic at work. Kids naturally resist any discipline, even though they need it. Children test boundaries even though children are profoundly comforted by having limits. Unless the husband and wife are absolutely on the same page, it is very easy for kids to triangulate between them. All parents have to deal with this problem.

Stepparenting is complicated by the fact that the parents are not naturally on equal footing in their relationship with the child. The biological parent already has a relationship with the child, and the stepparent is stepping into the flow in mid-stream. The children and the biological parent may already have developed an "us against the world" posture from living in what Dr. Phil calls, the "divorce foxhole," with all its stress. The biological parent can become protective toward the child, which is fine in itself. But if that protectiveness takes the form of shielding the child from any unpleasantness, including unpleasant consequences of their own behavior, the child can end up controlling the family with his "hurt" feelings. Statements such as "You aren't my REAL dad" or "you aren't REALLY my mom," become loaded weapons in the family. A vindictive child can use these wounding words as a plausible excuse for that all-too-typical resistance.

Dr. Phil handles this material very gingerly, sensitively and without judgment. But he makes it clear that being a stepparent is a genuine challenge. Reading the chapter on single-parent families with an open mind, leads inevitably to the conclusion that marriage makes it easier to be a good parent. If you are married to your child's other parent, and are on good working terms with him or her, raising successful children is going to be much easier and more straightforward. The happy talk we have been given that "children of divorce do just fine" is simply untrue. Dr. Phil does not come right out and bang the reader over the head. But the conclusion is almost impossible to avoid: successfully blending a family requires a lot of work.

Pastors should consider giving this chapter to couples contemplating divorce. Dr. Phil might help these struggling couples see that divorce won't necessarily solve every problem they now face. As parents, they will still have to interact with each other, even after divorce. Sometimes, brand new problems emerge while old problems are simply transferred to a different arena.

I have often thought that if people worked as hard at making marriage work as they do at making divorce work, they might stay married. With a more accurate image of how much effort stepparenting really takes, people might be inclined to work harder at keeping their marriages together. Dr. Phil's new book, *Family First,* is just the thing to give them that dose of reality.

Originally published: To The Source
January 20, 2005

available on-line at http://www.tothesource.org/1_19_2005/1_19_2005.htm - Reprinted with permission

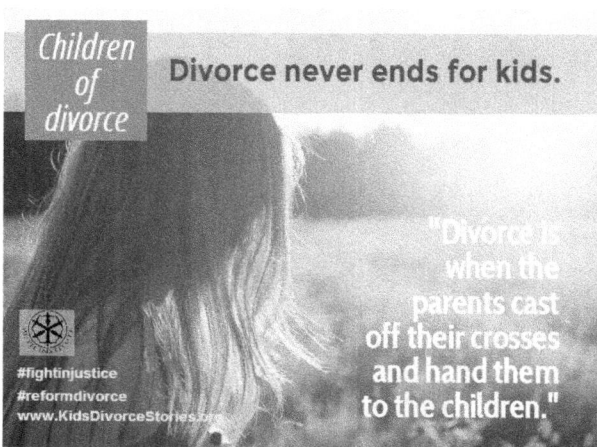

SECTION G
DIVORCE

~ 27 ~

A Response to Keith Ablow

ELEBRITY THERAPIST AND "LIFE coach" Dr. Keith Ablow just jumped on the "let's get the government out of the marriage business" bandwagon. I have been writing against the "privatizing marriage" mantra, going all the way back to 2005. I do not wish to rehearse those arguments here. But Dr. Ablow's contribution to this unfortunate genre is doubly regrettable. He is, first of all, deeply mistaken about the government's role in discouraging people from marriage. As a psychiatrist, he has no particular expertise in policy analysis, and I am sorry to say, it shows. My second regret about his foray into policy analysis is that he forsakes the area of his greatest expertise, namely, helping people live happier lives. His proposal to "get the government out of the marriage business" substitutes an easy exit strategy for the genuine work of building up marriage and family relationships.

Dr. Ablow claims that government intrusion is the cause of marriage decline because marriage amounts to signing a "draconian contract with the state to manage the division of your estate in the event of a divorce." Now he is certainly correct that under the current divorce regime, the family court micro-manages people's private lives. But his argument is completely backwards. He has no explanation for why people are less inclined to marry now, and why government is more intrusive now than in say, 1960. I can answer that: no-fault divorce.

California instituted the first "no-fault" divorce in 1968, with other states quickly following suit. The state no longer recognized marriage as a lifelong union, dissolvable only for cause. Under no-fault, either party could get divorced for any reason or no reason. The current "marriage contract," if you want to call it that, is less binding than a contract to purchase a home or to take delivery for a load of concrete. For sure, it is easier to end a marriage than for the L.A. Unified School District to fire a tenured teacher.

Most importantly, the legal change to the no-fault regime created unilateral divorce: The state now permits one party to break the marriage contract, regardless of the wishes of the other. This means that the divorce has to be enforced against the reluctant spouse. Somebody has to be separated from the joint assets of the marriage, most often, the family home and the children. The coercive machinery of the state is wheeled into place. The state begins the micromanaging of divorcing couples that Dr. Ablow rightly decries.

Dr. Ablow is correct that people are not getting married because they are afraid of divorce, including the state's involvement in their post-divorce lives. State governments undermine marriage by siding with the least committed spouse. Unilateral divorce was a policy change that just happened to increase the power of the state over people's lives. No-fault, unilateral divorce is the policy that ought to be reversed. That is not "getting the government out of the marriage business."

But Dr. Ablow's ill-advised foray into policy analysis is not the least of the problems with his article. He comments, in an off-hand way, that in his clinical observations, "the vast majority of married people consider their unions a source of pain, not pleasure, and that too few of them are equipped with the psychological and behavioral tools to achieve true intimacy or maintain real passion." Translation: People don't have good enough relationship skills to get and stay married, so let's give them an easier way out.

This statement is both illogical and appalling.

It is illogical because a therapist typically treats people who are having problems. Happily married people don't usually go to a therapist. He really shouldn't draw conclusions about the "vast majority of married people," based on a sample of clients in his own practice.

But suppose his clients really and truly don't have good relationship skills. His job as a life coach is precisely to give them those tools. It is appalling that he abandons that field, where he undoubtedly has something to contribute. Instead, he goes off on a tangent of abolishing marriage as a public institution. His policy proposal accommodates the present instability of marriage, when he should be leading the charge to combat it.

But, Dr. Ablow, isn't it your clinical observation that people actually want to get married and stay married? Don't people want intimacy and passion? And, don't children want and deserve parents who remain committed to each other?

This is where our current debate over the definition of marriage has led us. A noted psychiatrist joins the parade of people celebrating a cockamamie scheme for destroying marriage as an object of public concern. In the process, he is diverted from the serious business of helping people develop their capacity for love and relationship.

What a loss.

Originally published: National Review Online
December 29, 2011

Available on-line at http://www.nationalreview.com/home-front/286804/response-keith-ablow/
jennifer-roback-morse - Reprinted with permission

Natural marriage reflects the natural reality of the human body, of human reproduction, and the needs of children.

#1m1w
#naturalmarriage
www.RuthNewsletter.org

~ 28 ~

Striving for the Marriage Ideal: What Straight Divorce has to do with Gay 'Marriage'

P UBLIC OPINION POLLS SHOW that the vast majority of Americans oppose legalizing same-sex marriage. Yet that same public seems unwilling to go to the mat over the issue. What accounts for this reticence? I believe that the issue of divorce is lurking in the background of the debate.

Most Americans consider no-fault divorce a done-deal: feminists have effectively trashed the dreaded 1950's when divorce was considered a scandal. Few public opinion leaders are willing to link divorce to the arguments for heterosexual marriage. But we can't win the fight for heterosexual marriage without confronting the issue of divorce. Far from being a losing strategy, we can only win if we bring the divorce issue out of the closet.

Divorce is in the background of the gay marriage debate in at least three ways. First, gay marriage is the end of the trend that no-fault divorce began. The legal innovation of unilateral divorce began to reduce marriage to nothing but a temporary association of individuals. If marriage is merely a free association of individuals, there is no principled reason to exclude gay couples, or even larger groupings of sexual partners. The permanence of marriage was one of the key features that distinguished it from an ordinary contract.

Second, the high divorce rate and the resulting non-permanence of marriage made the institution of marriage more attractive to same-sex couples than it otherwise would be. If marriage still meant one to a customer for life, I seriously doubt that we'd be hearing about same-sex marriage today. Gay couples evidently have a more relaxed concept of both permanence and fidelity than do heterosexual couples. Gay activists would be much less likely to invest time and energy working for the right to marry, if divorce were available only for adultery or cruelty.

Most importantly, the high divorce rate has made it difficult to articulate opposition to gay marriage. People who have been divorced may feel hypocritical if they voice opposition to a system they felt they had to use. People who secretly fear they may need

139

a divorce someday are reluctant to bad-mouth the easy availability of divorce. People who are not confident in their own ability to keep their marriage together for a lifetime, won't speak out
against the culture of divorce. A significant subset of such people
will be reluctant to voice their opposition to gay marriage. People
who have lost confidence in marriage as an institution of exclu-
sivity and permanence are simply not going to have the heart for
a fight over gay marriage.

Gay activists instinctively know this. It is surprising how often
the topic of straight divorce comes up in the discussion of gay
marriage. The arguments go something like this: "No-fault divorce
has cut the link between marriage and permanence. Everyone accepts this. Easy divorce has also called into question the idea that
marriage is an institution for the good of the kids. A society that
accepts unilateral divorce is a society that is willing to sacrifice
the welfare of children to the comfort and happiness of adults, at
least to some extent. Since straight people are unwilling to give
up no-fault divorce, you can't very well claim that heterosexual
marriage is about permanence and children. So how can you justify excluding gays from marriage?"

This rhetorical move ends the argument. The opponent of gay
marriage is cowed into silence, for fear of being viewed either as
a hypocrite or a bigot. But we need not be shamed into silence
on this point. It is just that the alternative response requires us
to look the divorce issue squarely in the face.

Admit that unilateral divorce has undermined marriage. Agree
that straight people have already done a lot of harm to marriage.
The divorce rate is too high. Our attitude toward divorce is too
casual. Current law often does reward irresponsible behavior, on
the part of men and women alike.

We need to work to change all that. We don't have to accept unilateral divorce as a fixed feature of the universe. Divorce, even
when people think it is the only way, is painful and difficult for
men, women and children. Current divorce law allows people to
divorce for any reason or no reason, so lots of marriages dissolve
against the wishes of one person. Many divorced people in our
country could be described as reluctantly divorced.

When people have gone through a divorce, their response is not,
"hey that was fun. Let's do that again." No one aspires to have
their children get divorced when they grow up. People would certainly prefer to learn how to avoid divorce. Figuring out how to
live more comfortably with the person you married; figuring out

how to keep love more actively alive; making a wiser choice of partner in the first place: all these areas need work. Individuals and institutions, laws and customs, all have room for constructive change. And society needs to reform itself in all these ways, regardless of what gay people do or don't do, regardless of what the law says or doesn't say about gay marriage.

Of course, there is much more to be said about gay marriage, and about divorce, too, for that matter. But let's not kid ourselves. The current demand for homosexual marriage and the sad prevalence of heterosexual divorce are part and parcel of the same trend toward reducing marriage to a loose association of sexual partners. All of us need for marriage to be more than that.

Originally published: Breakpoint
May 4, 2006

Available on-line at: http://www.breakpoint.org/component/content/article/71-features/1708-striving-for-the-marriage-ideal - Reprinted with permission

~ 29 ~

The Superstition of Divorce
in a Holiday Movie

POPULAR CULTURE HAS A way of reflecting the anxieties and ambiguities of our age, sometimes without quite meaning to. Christmas 2008's bit of holiday eye candy, Four Christmases, illustrates the anxiety around insecure relationships, across the generations. The title comes from the visits that a happily un- married yuppie couple must make to their two sets of divorced parents. But the movie could be called The Superstitions of Di- vorce. It strips away the lies we tell ourselves to justify our rejec- tion of one another.

The Girlfriend, Reese Witherspoon, and Boyfriend, Vince Vaughn, each have to visit both of their divorced parents. We first have the Redneck Christmas, with Boyfriend's father. Then, we have the Sleazy Christmas with Girlfriend's mother, who is preoccupied with her own new boyfriend.

But not so preoccupied that she can't fawn all over Boyfriend.

Not only does she come on to Boyfriend, but so do all the other women in the family, including Girlfriend's aunts, her sister and even Gram-Gram. The third stop is a Hippie Christmas with Boy- friend's mother, who has taken up with his old school chum. Evi- dently, this is not her first love interest since her divorce.

All these stops along the way illustrate the impact of divorce, gen- eration by generation. The parents believe "If only I could dump spouse No. 1 and find someone better, all my problems would be solved." The adult children, Reese Witherspoon and Vince Vaughn, are afraid of commitment and intimacy. Even the grandchildren show scars: In one particularly ridiculous scene, we learn that one of the grandsons has a habit of stripping off his clothes and running away naked when he's upset.

Not a one of these first three parents has learned a thing from their divorces. Boyfriend and Girlfriend are not deceived by their parents' efforts to absolve themselves: They still have the same problems and crazy behavior. The new love interest doesn't solve their problems.

Over the course of their day together with their parents, Boyfriend

143

and Girlfriend each come to see more than they had known, and perhaps wanted to know, about the other. They aren't so much a couple as a pair of singles. Their life resembles what the Marriage Encounter folks call "The Married Singles Lifestyle." They come to realize this as they watch Boyfriend's brother and his wife: The rough-hewn redneck couple has a more intimate relationship than the "sophisticated" yuppie couple.

The real surprise of the movie comes during the car ride between Hippie Christmas and Girlfriend's father's house.

The Reese Witherspoon character makes a speech that could have come out of a natural family planning class or a theology of the body seminar. In the process of telling Boyfriend that she thinks she would like to have children someday, she tells him they have been holding out on each other.

"We have been setting so many boundaries and limits on our relationship. I want to be in a relationship that goes where it needs to go. We've been trying to protect ourselves. We've been acting on our fears." The audience sees, along with her, that her boyfriend's nonstop chatter does not add up to intimacy. Their money and their fancy vacations do not amount to real friendship.

Only when we get to the fourth Christmas, with Jon Voight as Girlfriend's father, do we begin to see anything like repentance, regrets or personal growth. He speaks wistfully of the fact that he has learned something from his multiple divorces.

The other characters seem not to have noticed that they themselves are a bit flaky and just might be difficult to live with. It is at this last house that some closure and healing comes. This pair of parents has a flawed but still genuine reconciliation.

"It took me several divorces to realize how many years I have spent lying to my family. I would give anything to get those years back." True humility: He is not blaming anyone but himself. Not surprisingly, the Jon Voight character is the most human and the most appealing of all the four parents.

Also not surprisingly, it is at her father's house that Girlfriend finds both acceptance and redemption. Her father was never taken in by any of the illusions the couple had created around themselves. And Boyfriend comes to realize that their life together, fun though it may be, is emotionally limited. He becomes willing to commit himself just a little to Girlfriend.

Mind you, I don't necessarily recommend that you go see this movie: It contains more unnecessary vulgarity than it needs to make its point.

Besides, the movie is unavailable now. But if you have already seen Four Christmases, or if it comes around your house on DVD next Christmas, understand that this film is a generation's attempt to come to grips with its own contradictions.

© National Catholic Register

---

*Originally published: National Catholic Register
March 13, 2009*

Available on-line at: http://www.ncregister.com/site/article/the_superstition_of_divorce_in_a_holiday_movie/ - Reprinted with permission

SECTION H
HOOK-UP
CULTURE

~ 30 ~

A Rubber Ideology

THE UPROAR OVER PRESIDENT Bush's appointment of a prominent abstinence advocate to head up the federal Office of Population Affairs reveals as much about the screamers as it does about the scream-ee. Dr. Eric Keroack advocates abstinence as the most reliable method of pregnancy and STD prevention. His critics are outraged that Bush would appoint someone who isn't all about contraception to head up the federal office responsible for family planning. These critics don't seem to realize that the same office also oversees the federal abstinence programs. They seem to think that only an empty-headed ideologue could promote abstinence. But there is also an ideology surrounding contraception.

I call it "condomism." This is the belief that all problems surrounding sexual activity could be solved with enough contraception. Some adherents, such as contributors to the recent special issue of *The Lancet,* go even further. They believe that we could end world hunger and save the environment, if only we had enough condoms. Here are some of the tenets of condomism:

» Every person capable of giving meaningful consent is entitled to unlimited sexual activity.
» All negative consequences of sexual activity can be controlled through the use of contraception. Sexually Transmitted Diseases can be controlled through the use of condoms. The probability of pregnancy can be eliminated through contraception, properly used.
» No one is required to give birth to a baby, in the event of pregnancy. Abortion, for any reason or no reason, at any time during pregnancy, is an absolute entitlement.
» Any negative consequences of sexual activity that cannot be handled by contraception or abortion are not worth talking about.

The controversy over Keroack's views on bonding during sexual activity illustrates this last point. Evidently, Keroack has given lectures in which he claims that there are long-term emotional costs to non-marital sexual activity. According to Amanda Schaffer, writing in *Slate,* Keroack said this: "People who have misused

149

their sexual faculty and become bonded to multiple persons will diminish the power of oxytocin to maintain a permanent bond with an individual."

Schaffer cites this as an example of outrageous claims that Keroack makes to "scare the bejesus out of kids to convince them to remain abstinent." But I think her outrage reveals the zeal of condomist ideology. No known contraceptive method eliminates the risk of being emotionally wounded by inappropriate sex. Therefore, condomists must stamp out discussion of negative consequences of sexual activity that can't be handled with contraception.

Schaffer cites as evidence a recent review article on oxytocin. But "The Neuroscience of Affiliation," by Drs. Jennifer Bartz and Eric Hollander,[1] only bears indirectly on the question at hand. According to Bartz and Hollander, "Overall, the findings from the studies of healthy humans parallel those from animal studies and point to the role of oxytocin in stress response and in enhancing social affiliation; however, the underlying mechanisms are not yet well understood."

More to the point: Look at what we do know for sure. We know for sure that oxytocin promotes bonding and affiliation, even though we don't know everything we'd like to know about how the mechanism works. We know that sexual activity promotes oxytocin production, especially though not exclusively in women. We know that young people with early sexual initiation and multiple sexual partners are less likely to be in a stable happy relationship at age 30.[2] And we know that sexual activity, particularly casual sex[3] and multiple partners, increases the risk of depression for teenage females.

I have presented material on sexual behavior and the physiology of attachment many times. I have gotten a pretty good feel for how audiences react. I use a phrase from Theresa Crenshaw, author of The Alchemy of Love and Lust: The oxytocin response can create "an involuntary chemical commitment." When I explain that women are particularly prone to get an oxytocin-generated feeling of attachment, the room gets very quiet, as people start thinking

---

1   **Hormonal Behavior.** 2006 Nov;50(4):518-28. Epub 2006 Aug 1. http://www. ncbi.nlm.nih.gov/pubmed/16884725?dopt=Abstract

2   Ralph Rector, et.al. "Harmful Effects of Early Sexual Activity and Multiple Sexual Partners Among Women: A Book of Charts," **Heritage Foundation, WebMemo** 303, June 26, 2003.

3   "Which comes first in adolescence—sex and drugs or depression?" Hallfors DD, Waller MW, Bauer D, Ford CA, Halpern CT. **American Journal of Preventative Medicine.** 2005 Oct;29(3):163-70. Available on-line at: http:// www.ncbi.nlm.nih.gov/pubmed/16168864?dopt=AbstractPlus

back over their experiences. Some people do not welcome this information. But most are relieved: They see an explanation for some of the seemingly inexplicable things they've done and impossible situations they have gotten themselves into.

People have told me that they now understood why they found it difficult to break off with a cohabiting partner whom they knew was not really right for them. I've had counselors tell me that the oxytocin connection helps them understand why sexually active couples whom they can see are incompatible, nevertheless get married. I've had young people tell me that they were glad they had heard me talk when they were 22, instead of much later. They felt I had spared them a lot of grief.

Whether Keroack's string of inferences or causal chain is exactly correct I cannot say. But it is beyond doubt that his general conclusion is absolutely correct: The physiology of attachment is undoubtedly part of the explanation for why non-marital sex is a risk factor for later relationship difficulties. He is drawing a perfectly logical conclusion from the available evidence.

And besides, what is the alternative position that Keroack's critics would promote? That unattached sex is completely costless, as long as it is safely contracepted? That young people should feel perfectly free to have as many sexual encounters as they want, provided they use a condom?

This is why I say condomism is an ideological position. Any problem that can't be solved with contraception is not worth talking about.

I cannot vouch for everything Keroack and any organization he's been involved with have ever said or done. But it is not scaring the bejesus out of people to inform them of the substantial emotional risks associated with casual sex.

Originally published: National Review Online
December 5, 2006

Available on-line at: http://www.nationalreview.com/articles/219415/rubber-ideology/jennifer-roback-morse - Reprinted with permission

SECTION H
HOOK-UP CULTURE

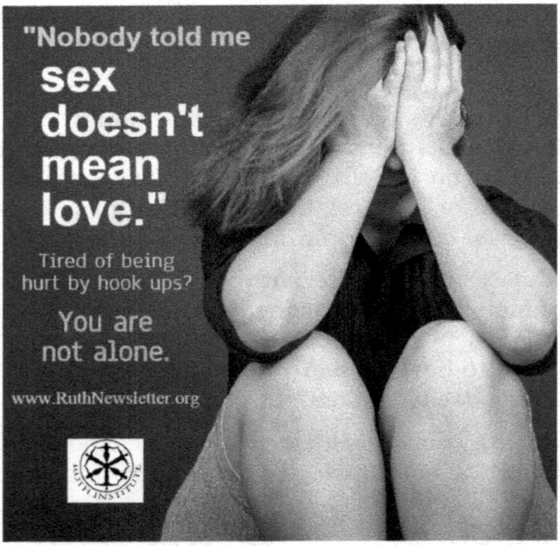

~ 31 ~

Sex, Lies and Videotape

A FTER ANY SUICIDE, THE survivors search their souls for its meaning and what they might have done to prevent it. The recent tragedy of a young man diving off the George Washington Bridge after his roommate posted a sexual video of him is no exception. Advocates of greater acceptance of same sex sexual activity have seized upon this case as ammunition for their cause. But I believe viewing this incident through a wider lens will benefit young people generally, not just those who experience same sex attraction. For the last 40 years, adult society has steadily pummeled young people with the message that "sex is no big deal." This case proves once and for all, that this claim is false. Adult society should stop sending this message, in all its forms.

Why did this promising young man kill himself? Evidently, he negotiated with this roommate to have the private use of their room for a sexual encounter with another guy. His roommate made a video of him engaged in sex and posted it on the internet. The young guy killed himself.

Now, if sex is really "just a normal bodily function," why on earth would he be so distraught that he would end his life? Maybe he wasn't embarrassed about the sexual act itself, only about the violation of his privacy. But what if his roommate had caught him in the act of picking his nose or going to the bathroom? It strains the imagination to believe that he would have killed himself over the display of these "normal bodily functions." If sex is really "just a recreational activity," would anyone kill himself over a video showing him playing baseball or checkers or video games?

Maybe he was afraid people would not accept him, that he would be teased, specifically because he was engaged in a homosexual act. But this assumes that students at a university like Rutgers actually care. Sex is no big deal, remember? Whether you're doing it with a guy or a girl, no problem, as long as you both consent and you use "protection."

Actually, this particular student killed himself before much teasing could even begin from this particular incident. But let's say he was correct, and that he could reasonably anticipate sexual teasing. Parenthetically, let's note that sexual teasing is not a specifically "gay" problem. Several girls have committed suicide over the teasing fallout from "sexting." These girls endured months of teasing and harassment before they killed themselves.

Gay or straight, male or female, these incidents raise a fundamental question about the official position of our sexual culture. Is it really true that "sex is no big deal?"

The sensitivity of these students to sexual teasing as opposed to other forms of teasing, the fact that we all intuitively know that this form of teasing is uniquely painful, the fact that even bullies, insensitive thugs though they may be, instinctively hone in on the sexual aspects of a person's life as the most vulnerable: all these things point to one simple truth. Sex is a big deal. We have not succeeded in talking ourselves out of this, in spite of enormous cultural efforts to do so. In fact, let's not mince words: we have faced 40 years worth of intense propaganda trying to break down any sense of sexual decorum.

I'm sure the people promoting these messages have their reasons. Perhaps they wish to convince themselves and others that there is no basis for judging sexual acts or the people who participate in them. Perhaps they wish to overcome sexual shame, thinking that we will be happier if all that baggage can be jettisoned. But the persistent sensitivity of young people like these suggests that sexual reticence may run more deeply in the human psyche than we have supposed, and that purging it entirely from the human soul may not be possible.

This doesn't necessarily prove that any particular code of sexual conduct is the correct one. It surely does suggest that it is rational to ask the question of what constitutes the sexual good for men and women. Reasonable people may disagree. But we are doing ourselves and our young people no favor by telling them there is no such thing as better or worse sexual behavior.

It is time we admit the truth that each of us knows deep in our hearts: sex is more than a pleasurable instinct. Sex is deeply meaningful, so much so, that we may be forgiven for calling it "sacred." It is time we stop kidding ourselves.

Originally published: MercatorNet.com
October 11, 2010

Available on-line at: http://www.mercatornet.com/articles/view/sex_lies_and_videotape - Reprinted with permission

~ 32 ~

Desperate Grandmas and Satisfied Housewives

OLDER WOMEN WHO HAVE chosen since their early years to forgo lifelong relationships in pursuit of casual, non-commital sex are actually writing about it, and quite explicitly at that! Wisdom did not come with age for these grandmas, who still haven't figured out that they made the wrong decision long ago.

Baby Boomer feminists invented casual sex as a lifelong lifestyle choice. Erica Jong's *Fear of Flying* elevated casual sex from the impulse purchase of randy teenagers to a carefully considered strategy for a lifetime. Marriage is for fuddy-duddies. True freedom means to be unencumbered by human relationships, always open to new possibilities. Now that this generation is about to retire, they are giving us a glimpse into how this investment program worked out for them

They are writing their memoirs. God help us all.

Kay Hymowitz recently reviewed a few memoirs for a *City Journal* article called "Desperate Grandmas." The grandmas are desperate to show that they are *Still Doing It,* and that it is *Better Than I Ever Expected.* The author of a particularly exhibitionist book called *A Round-Heeled Woman* actually advertised in the *New York Review of Books* for lovers to use as the basis for her book. "Before I turn 67–next March– I would like to have a lot of sex with a man I like. If you want to talk first, Trollope works for me."

Gosh. When I'm 67, I expect to be having a lot of sex with a man I like, unless something untoward happens to Mr. Morse. I won't even have to advertise.

As for Erica Jong's latest novel, *Seducing the Demon,* Hymowitz describes it as "deeply embarrassing." Ms. Jong doesn't seem to realize that no one cares about her orgasms.

I certainly hope the *City Journal* gave Kay Hymowitz hazard pay for reading this nonsense.

She hits the nail on the head in her analysis of what is wrong with these women's approach to aging and sexuality. It is "their enthusiastic display of that chronic boomer disease: narcissism."

157

Their excessive focus on the self has made it almost impossible for these women to form real relationships. By searching endlessly for self-actualization, they missed the growth that is only possible through self-giving. They spent their lives "finding themselves," and never find anyone else.

But every "yes" is a "no" to its opposite. By saying "yes" to casual sex, easy divorce, and literary exhibitionism, these hip grandmas have said "no" to marriage and all the benefits it brings. Most happily married people don't need to take out advertisements for sex. Nor do they take pleasure in writing books describing their sex lives to anonymous readers.

Married couples have more sex and more satisfying sex than singles or divorced people. In *The Case for Marriage: Why Married People are Happier, Healthier and Better Off Financially,* Maggie Gallagher and Linda Waite cite the social science research on this subject: 42% of married women find sex "extremely emotionally satisfying," compared with only 31% of those single women who had a regular sex partner. And of those women who have never married, 30% had no sex at all in the past year, compared with a mere 3% of married women.

I am of approximately the same generation as the Desperate Grandmas. But I am not desperate. Far from it. Why? Because I am still married to the same man I married in 1984. Marriage helped us overcome our all-too-human tendency to self-absorption. We had to learn to accommodate each other, care about each other. Heck, sometimes it was an effort to even notice each other.

It wasn't just our relationship that coaxed us out of our self-centeredness. Our kids helped, too. We have two kids. We have had eight foster kids. They drew us out of our self-absorption, quite against our will, I might add. I think my husband will concur that we each could have gone through life thinking My Life is All About Me.

Instead of a book called, *Still Doing It,* maybe I should write a book called, *Still Doing It (With the Same Man!).* Or maybe, *Better Than We Ever Expected,* instead of *Better Than I Ever Expected,* to indicate that our sex life is not about me, but about us.

The sexual revolution tried to give us sex without relationship. But sex is fundamentally relational. No wonder the Baby Boomer grandmas are so desperate.

The generation of twenty-something women has a choice about what path to follow. Which will it be: sex without relationship, or lifelong married love? We Baby Boomers have made our choices. Now the choice is yours.

Originally published: National Review On-line
September 19, 2006

Available on-line at: http://www.nationalreview.com/articles/218692/desperate-grandmas-satisfied-housewives-jennifer-roback-morse - Reprinted with permission

SECTION H
HOOK-UP CULTURE

~ 33 ~

Unprotected: Students Exposed to Disease and Heartache

CAMPUS PSYCHIATRIST IS DRIVEN to write about the way students' bodies and souls are sacrificed to the sexual ideology reigning in colleges.

It is a continuing mystery how advanced Western societies can, with a straight face, declare that trans fats should be banned (as in New York City) but at the same time, ignore the health risks associated with non-monogamous sexual activity. Finally, someone with authority dares to speak out. Her name is Dr. Miriam Grossman but she called herself Dr. Anonymous when she wrote, *Unprotected: A Campus Psychiatrist Reveals How Political Correctness in her Profession Endangers Every Student.* As a psychiatrist at the University of California, Los Angeles (UCLA), she has treated thousands of college students over the past ten years. If you have a loved one in college, you owe it to them to read *Unprotected to* find out what is really going on.

Adults think they are teaching the young to be non-judgmental, but this translates into the young having no basis for making judgements about what is good for them. Although there is plenty of evidence that sex without commitment is emotionally and physically harmful, this evidence is carefully concealed from the young. So even while they are told to make their own decisions, the adults around them systematically understate the harms of non-marital sex. The author is especially effective because she dramatizes general points with the stories of particular individual students who typify a problem.

She tells of Brian, a gay student who came to her because he wanted medication to help him stop smoking. During the course of the session it transpired that he and his boyfriend often pick up other men. "It's hard to be monogamous," he explained. Neither Brian nor his boyfriend use condoms for protection. Neither has ever been tested for HIV.

The author reviews her responsibilities toward patients suspected of having tuberculosis. The law expects the doctor to test students at-risk of TB. If the skin test is positive, she is required to give him a chest X-ray. If the combination of skin test and chest

X-ray point to TB, the doctor is required to report him to the Department of Health within a day. Yet for students at-risk for HIV, she can only recommend testing and discourage unsafe activities. A man from Mars would conclude that we are more concerned about the health of TB patients than of HIV patients.

A student named Heather is referred for unexplained depression. After discarding numerous possible explanations, including academic pressure, poor health, death of a pet, the doctor asks Heather whether she has had any changes in her relationships. Heather thinks it over, "Well, I can think of one thing: since Thanksgiving, I've had a 'friend with benefits.' And actually I'm kind of confused about that... I want to spend more time with him, and do stuff like go shopping or see a movie. That would make it a friendship for me. But he says no, because if we do those things, then in his opinion we'd have a relationship, and that's more than he wants. And I'm confused because it seems like I don't get the 'friend' part, but he still gets the 'benefits'.

The author recounts the evidence that sexually active teenage girls are about three times more likely to be depressed and to have attempted suicide than girls who were not sexually active. She also recounts the evidence that women's physiology creates this vulnerability. Women secrete a hormone called oxytocin during sexual activity, and while nursing a baby. Oxytocin promotes bonding, trust and relaxation. Mother Nature evidently is trying to get us to connect with our babies, and with our sex partners, who after all, might become the father to our children.

Oxytocin recently made an appearance in American politics. George Bush's appointment to the Office of Population Affairs actually believes in abstinence. The Life-Style Left discovered that Dr. Eric Keroack had once given a lecture in which he informed people about the bonding power of oxytocin. They went apoplectic, rather than confront the evidence on its own terms.

This refusal to face inconvenient facts cries out for explanation. One of the author's patients asked her, "Why, Doctor, do they tell you how to protect your body from herpes and pregnancy, but they don't tell you what it does to your heart?"

I have my own theory about this, which is completely complementary with the author's experience. Far from being sexually neutral, tolerant and non-judgmental, the Life-Style Left subscribes to a covert ideology. I call it Condomism. Its chief tenets are that sex is a private recreational activity with no moral or social significance. Unlimited sexual activity is an entitlement. There are no

162

harms associated with sex that cannot be controlled by condoms or other forms of contraception.

And if anyone complains about anything that can't be controlled by condoms, well, those complaints are not worth taking seriously. Getting attached to inappropriate sex partners? Never happens. Women's depression associated with uncommitted sex? Must be bad data. Post Traumatic Stress Disorder associated with abortion? A mere blip in the data, even though the author's back-of-the-envelope calculations show that if a mere 1 percent of post-abortive women develop PTSD symptoms, that amounts to 420,000 traumatized women. That's a lot of women to dismiss.

Unprotected is a bold and important book. Buy it. Read it. Pass it around. You may just save someone you love a lot of heartache.

Originally published: Mercatornet.com
January 11, 2007

Available on-line at: http://www.mercatornet.com/articles/view/unprotected_students_exposed_to_ disease_and_heartache - Reprinted with permission

SECTION I
VICTIMS OF THE
SEXUAL REVOLUTION

~ 34 ~

Taylor Swift: Another Victim of the Sexual Revolution

HE ENTERTAINMENT MEDIA ESTABLISHMENT, Gossip Division, is reporting that Taylor Swift gave her virginity to a man she thought was going to marry her. Three months later, she had a party for herself, and he didn't show up. This took place at Christmastime of 2010. I don't know exactly why The Entertainment Media Establishment, Gossip Division is reporting it now. Maybe Ms. Swift's handlers issued a new press release about it, to drum up publicity. Or something.

Pop star, yes, but also just a 20-year-old kid.

In any case, as the mother of a young woman about the same age as Taylor, I find the whole story heartbreaking. Some of the media outlets have been down-right catty towards this now 24-year-old young woman, over the years since she broke up with Jake. Philly.com calls her the "Miss Goodie Goodie of the pop community." The Huffington Post admitted that "for her part, Swift is devastated," but opined, "On the plus side, at least she's got some new material for her next album." Hollywood Life wants to know: "What do YOU think HollywoodLifers? Is Taylor right to diss Jake again? Should she and Harry reunite?"

The Entertainment Media Establishment, Gossip Division seems indifferent to the fact that Taylor was 20 years old when this happened. She was and to some extent remains, a vulnerable young woman. I'm guessing the authors of these catty columns about her are somewhat older than 20.

She was "saving herself for marriage." The guy convinced her to have sex with him. Shortly after, he ditched her.

Not mentioned in any of these stories: women tend to attach to their sex partners. We experience a surge of a hormone called oxytocin during sex. This hormone creates feelings of relaxation and connection. Men have fewer oxytocin receptors than women. This is why women so often connect more strongly after a sexual encounter than men do.

In fact, you could say that "casual sex" is not even possible for women. We tend to connect to our sex partners, whether we

167

mean to or not.

The Sexual Revolution told us that men and women are completely interchangeable. What men do, women are entitled to do.

The Sexual Revolution told us that sex is no big deal, a sterile recreational activity that doesn't hurt anyone, as long as you use a condom.

Tell that to Taylor Swift and all the other heartbroken young women who have cried themselves to sleep over relationships that meant more to them than to the guy.

As long as Taylor keeps cranking out the hit songs, no one really cares about her and her feelings and her future ability to sustain relationships.

I feel for this kid. I'm sorry if that sounds mother-hen-ish. But I can't help it. That is how I feel.

Originally published: Ruth Blog
June 8, 2014

On-line at: http://www.ruthblog.org/2014/06/08/taylor-swift-another-victim-of-the-sexual-revolution/

~ 35 ~

How the West's Fertility War Has Left Women at Risk

A review of *Unnatural Selection: Choosing Boys over Girls, and the Consequences of a World Full of Men* - Mara Hvistendahl

THIS BRAVE AND TIMELY book has many strengths and one glaring, but understandable, weakness. The strength of this book is the reporting. Mara Hvistendahl, a liberal, pro-choice feminist, painstakingly documents the catastrophic consequences of the worldwide "choice" for male babies: gender imbalance leading to prostitution, sex slavery, and male frustration and aggression. The weakness of this book is the political analysis. She doesn't understand how deeply *Roe v. Wade* changed American political culture, particularly within the conservative movement broadly conceived. But both these strengths and weaknesses work together to yield an honest and courageous book that should be read by anyone who considers himself (or herself) well informed.

Let's start with the strengths. Hvistendahl is a very honest reporter. She became aware of the gender-imbalance problem while living in China as a journalist. She recounts how she visited a grade-school classroom to write an article on the solar heating system being installed in the school. She found herself in a "classroom full of smiling boys. I was tempted to abandon the solar power article and interview the teachers about the school's population." That experience repeated itself so many times that she couldn't stand it anymore. Her journalist instincts required an investigation of the imbalanced sex ratio in Chinese society.

She found that the problem, however, is not unique to China, with its particularly high-pressure "one child policy" driving small family size. Hvistendahl found gender imbalances all around the world, not just in China or India. Albania, South Korea, Taiwan, Vietnam, parts of Singapore, all have experienced skewed sex ratios. The normal gender ratio at birth hovers around 105 boys for every 100 girls, with anything between 104 through 106 boys considered normal. The Caucasus countries of the former Soviet Union have badly skewed sex ratios. Azerbaijan has a sex ratio of 115 boys, Georgia 118, and Armenia, a whopping 120. The American journalist expected that the explanation would be sexist attitudes: in male-dominated societies, patriarchs prefer sons. But she found that women were just as likely to prefer sons, and as responsible for sex-selection abortion, as their husbands. She also found that urban elites, not the rural poor, pioneered the practice of sex-selection abortion.

WHERE TECHNOLOGY AND ABORTION MEET

The factors that give rise to gender imbalance are a mix of technology and economic development, layered over the top of traditionalist belief systems. Among the factors related to economic development, the first is a rapidly developing economy, and one with a health-care system mature enough so that prenatal screening is widely and cheaply available. Second, abortion is pervasive, available at low cost and free of social stigma. And finally, in societies with gender imbalances, the overall population is declining.

In pre-modern times, old sex stereotypes and preferences for sons drove families to continue having children until they have a son. Today, those preferences have not dissipated. New ultrasound technology makes it possible to detect the sex of the child in the womb. The modern custom is to abort the baby if it is a girl; if a boy, give it birth. No need to experience nine months of pregnancy, and all the trouble of delivery, for every baby you conceive. Just give birth to the ones you want and kill the others in utero. Hence, technology and the availability of abortion, not just a "patriarchal" preference for sons, have been driving the imbalance of the sexes. Traditional attitudes for the imbalance are far from the whole story. As an Indian obstetrician put it, "If people had a son simply because they wanted a son, girls would have disappeared from this country one thousand years ago."

Western population controllers were delighted with sex-selection abortion because it delivered a double whammy. Reducing the number of girls born reduces the numbers of future potential mothers. So getting the locals to "choose" sons over daughters using sex-selection abortion reduces both current and future populations. But unlike many of the population-control ideologues whom she covers, Hvistendahl never falls into the trap of believing that economic development requires abortion or population control. After all, the West, which is synonymous with "development," didn't require population control in order to grow economically. On the contrary, development came first; reduced family sizes came later.

The gender imbalance arose because of the push to cut birthrates and the prevalence of legal abortion. Both of these dubious factors were exported into developing countries by United Nations agencies in collaboration with elite American foundations. One might even say that the so-called experts of the West imposed these things on poor countries. The imported pressure to reduce overall fertility, combined with the general desire for sons, made the ultrasound technology irresistible.

YOUNG WOMEN AS CHATTEL

The consequences of the gender imbalance brought on by the Western war on fertility expose its bare brutality. French demographer Christophe Guilmoto estimates that roughly 163 million baby girls are missing in the world today. This is approximately the population of women in the United States. This magnitude of a sex-ratio imbalance means that when all these little boys grow up to be men, there will not be enough women for them all to marry.

No one to marry, explains Hvistendahl in riveting detail, means that men are older when they marry. They have to be better off financially in order to be an acceptable husband. Economists like Gary Becker predict that the skewed sex ratio benefits women, who become the scarce resource. Men have to compete for their attention. Yet Becker's theory doesn't account for the powerlessness of the young girl. Yes, she is a valuable resource. But she can't leverage that higher value unless her rights are socially and legally recognized. Without that protection, her value will be captured by someone with the power to protect his property rights in her and in her services, usually meaning her parents or her pimp. Her parents can use her value in the marriage market to extract the resources from her potential husband for themselves but not for her. Even worse, she may be kidnapped and trafficked into prostitution.

Hvistendahl recounts in sickening detail the lives of women shuttled from one place to another in a life of sex slavery. Women are scarce. Hence, so are their sexual services. The exclusive sharing of sexual intimacy with a husband in the protective bonds of marriage becomes more expensive than arrangements giving multiple men access to a single woman. Hence, prostitution, voluntary or otherwise, becomes lucrative as the demand for commercial sex increases. In addition, men without wives are more likely to become violent and commit crimes. Indeed, Hvistendahl shows that the gender-imbalance ratio is a better predictor of a region's crime rate than poverty. All these consequences, foisted on the poorer countries of the world by a population-control establishment that has yet to concede its errors, flow from the gender imbalance.

WHERE HVISTENDAHL NEEDS HELP

Now, the weakness of the book: Hvistendahl doesn't understand how profoundly *Roe v. Wade* transformed American politics. She identifies early population controllers—such as William Draper, the general who pushed for Uncle Sam to promote "family planning" in foreign policy during the Eisenhower years—as political "conservatives," as if they could be grouped with the Religious Right today. She doesn't understand how anti-communism—not social conservatism—animated conservatives of the Soviet era. Indeed, the 1973 Roe decision was still a generation away.

The fact is that the Religious Right is almost entirely a creation of *Roe v. Wade*. Prior to *Roe*, evangelical Protestants were not animated by politics because America was, for the most part, what we would now call a socially conservative country. Liberal Protestantism was a minority religious system confined to the elite leaders of the northern denominations but never reflected the sentiments of the Protestant rank-and-file. And Roman Catholics represented a solid Democratic voting bloc. The 1973 Supreme Court decision, however, drove many Catholics out of the Democratic party and into the GOP and, over time, drew evangelical Protestants into the political fray. Their shared opposition to abortion drove Catholics and evangelicals together and created a sense of mutual, if sometimes grudging respect. Neither group—then or now—has much in common with the anti-Communist population controllers whom Hvistendahl calls "conservative."

Nor does Hvistendahl understand how public policies pushing birth control eventually led to public policies favoring abortion. Yet the reason why greater access to contraception goes hand-in-hand with abortion, including sex-selection abortion, is not difficult to grasp. Separating sexual activity from reproduction is a powerful idea, seductive, superficially appealing with promises of fun and freedom without consequences. The idea begins with contraception. But simply preventing conception is not enough to fully separate sex from babies, because contraception sometimes fails. Even sterilization is perceived as too crude: once sterilized, always sterilized. Only

abortion satisfies the demand to completely separate sex from reproduction, while still keeping an open option for eventual conception.

We can call this brave new world the "abortion regime." Its appeal is superficially obvious. But the full brutality of the regime only becomes apparent with time. It takes time for the power of the idea of separating sex from conception to work its way through the social, economic, and legal systems. The emergence of sex-selection abortion on a widespread scale was not an immediately obvious consequence of unhinging sex from procreation. Yet the resulting gender imbalance, with all its problems so ably recounted by Hvistendahl, is just another cost of "choice."

To her credit, Hvistendahl is honest enough to realize that the rhetoric of choice and the politics of abortion are gravely culpable in creating the problems she documents. She notes in her prologue that she found herself agreeing with anti-abortion activists almost in spite of herself. She found herself "corresponding with public relations officers whose voice mail messages ended with 'God bless.'" Given that appeal, the pro-life movement should embrace Mara Hvistendahl and her fine book. The pro-life movement has become, after all, a women's movement and a youth movement. If Hvistendahl hangs around with us for a while, maybe she will come to see that it is possible to have a movement for women's empowerment that doesn't require the killing of small children.

Originally published: The Family in America
Summer 2011

Available on-line at: http://familyinamerica.org/journals/summer-2011/how-wests-fertility-war-has-left-women-risk/#.VKByuV4AKA - Reprinted with permission

Dr. Jennifer Roback Morse

Dr. Morse is the founder of the Ruth Institute, a non-profit organization committed to addressing the lies created by the Sexual Revolution over the past 50 years. She has authored three books and spoken around the globe regarding her theories on marriage, family and sexuality from a social and economic standpoint. She has engaged in debates and discussions with lawyers, professors, church prelates, elected officials and policy makers on the issues of natural marriage, humane feminism and demographic winter.

Dr. Morse earned her Ph.D. in Economics at the University of Rochester in 1980. She taught economics at Yale University and George Mason University. She has served as a Research Fellow for the Acton Institute for the Study of Religion and Liberty and has held fellowships at Stanford University's Hoover Institution, Cornell Law School, and the University of Chicago's economics department. She authored many scholarly articles in peer-reviewed journals and law reviews, such as the Journal of Political Economy, the Harvard Journal of Law and Public Policy, and the University of Chicago Law Review. She has written opinion and analysis pieces that appeared in such outlets as the Wall Street Journal, Forbes, Reason, Policy Review, National Review Online, and many others.

She is the author of *"Love and Economics: It Takes a Family to Raise a Village," "101 Tips for a Happier Marriage,"* and *"Smart Sex: Finding Life-long Love in a Hook-up World,"* as well as numerous pamphlets and tracts on issues, including *"The Government's Duty to Marriage"* and *"The Socialist Attack on the Family."* A noted international speaker, she has been featured at the World Meeting of Families in Valencia, Spain in 2006, sponsored by the *Pontifical Council on the Family; the Love Singapore Momentum Conference* in 2014; and as a guest on Fox News, CNN and EWTN, among others.

Dr. Morse was named one of the *"Catholic Stars of 2013"* by *Our Sunday Visitor* – a list that included Pope Francis and Pope Benedict XVI.

Over the years, Dr. Morse observed the ever de-stabilizing sexual situation on university campuses and the harm it has caused. She founded the Ruth Institute in 2008 as a vehicle to help student leaders understand why a free society requires socially conservative values, with marriage being the centerpiece around which the rest revolve. Much of the education provided by the Ruth Institute is academic and scientific rather than theological, drawing heavily from economics, law, social science, psychology, physiology, and other disciplines. Dr. Morse has developed a close network of like-minded scientists, scholars, and professionals from these disciplines who work with the Institute to further its mission.

Dr. Morse and her husband are parents of an adopted child, a birth child, eight foster children and now a goddaughter. She and her husband are keenly aware of the pressures facing emerging adults today.